Who's COMING TO DINNER?

Jesus Made Known in the Breaking of Bread

Robert C. Morgan

ABINGDON PRESS

Nashville

WHO'S COMING TO DINNER?
Jesus Made Known in the Breaking of Bread

This book is printed on recycled, acid-free paper.

Library of Congress Cataloging-in-Publication Data

MORGAN, ROBERT C., 1933-
   Who's coming to dinner? : Jesus made known in the breaking of bread / Robert C. Morgan.
      p.   cm.
   ISBN 0-687-45344-5 (alk. paper)
   1. Jesus Christ—Person and offices. 2. Dinners and dining in the Bible. I. Title.
BT205.M66   1991
232.9'5—dc20   91-42509
                                                                            CIP

Scripture quotations marked "Phillips" are from *The New Testament in Modern English,* revised edition, by J. B. Phillips. Copyright © 1958, 1960, 1972 and are reprinted with permission of Macmillan Publishing Co., Inc.

Scripture quotations marked KJV are from the King James Version of the Bible.

Scripture quotations marked NEB are from *The New English Bible.* © The Delegates of the Oxford University Press and The Syndics of the Cambridge University Press 1961, 1970. Reprinted by permission.

Scripture quotations marked NRSV are from the New Revised Standard Version Bible, copyright © 1989, by the Division of Christian Education of the National Council of the Churches of Christ in the United States of America.

Scripture quotations, where noted, are the author's paraphrase of the Bible.

MANUFACTURED IN THE UNITED STATES OF AMERICA

To my friends,

Mac and Mary Ann McCarty

whose generosity and vision have made it
possible for hundreds
of Mississippi United Methodist ordinands
to experience the "fifth gospel" firsthand.

Contents

Acknowledgments..9

Foreword..11

  1. *Made Known in the Breaking of Bread:*
The NATURE of God Made Known.......................................15

  2. *Look Who's Coming to Dinner!:*
SALVATION Made Known.. 23

  3. *The World's Most Famous Barbecue:*
FORGIVENESS Made Known... 31

  4. *Serving People and Tables:*
SERVANTHOOD Made Known.. 43

  5. *Putting First Things First:*
His PRIORITIES Made Known... 55

  6. *Plenty Good Room at My Father's Table:*
JUSTICE Made Known...67

  7. *How Much Is "So Much"?:*
LOVE Made Known...77

  8. *The Place Jesus Has Prepared for Us:*
ETERNAL LIFE Made Known.. 87

  9. *Basic Table Manners According to Jesus:*
HUMILITY Made Known..99

  10. *Interrupted Supper:*
His COMPASSION Made Known.. 109

Contents

11. *Called to Be the Life of the Party:*
His HUMOR Made Known..117

12. *More Than Bread and Wine:*
The NEW COVENANT Made Known.....................................129

13. *A Second Helping:*
GRACE Made Known...137

14. *Food to Go:*
Our MISSION Made Known..149

Acknowledgments

*D*r. William Graham "Pop" Echols, the Director of the Wesley Foundation at the University of Alabama for more than thirty years, first convinced me that I needed to study in Jerusalem and Galilee. Since that first time, I have been privileged to make several study trips to the Middle East.

Most of my research and writing for this book occurred during extended study leaves in Jerusalem and Galilee. Dr. James Ridgeway, the Executive Director of Educational Opportunities, afforded me unlimited support and encouragement. I am grateful to a number of the faculty members of Hebrew University and the staff of the Jerusalem Center for Biblical Studies for allowing me to study with them. They introduced me to Ernest Renan's concept of the "fifth gospel"—the customs, culture, geography, feasts and language that the biblical writers assumed their readers understood. To become familiar with the "fifth gospel" is to experience and appreciate a new understanding of the Scriptures.

I owe a special debt of gratitude to Dr. James Fleming, the Director of Biblical Resources Study Center in Jerusalem. His teaching, along with my study and travel in Israel, have influenced much of what I share with you in this book.

The late Dr. Albert E. Barnett, professor of New Testament at the Candler School of Theology, Emory University, was the first teacher who enabled me to see the clear relevancy of the gospel to the society we live in. His colleague, the late Dr. Frederick Prussner, made the Old Testament come alive for me.

There are a number of persons who helped me write this book. First of all is my wife, Martha, who encouraged, harassed, and pampered me while I was writing the manuscript. She challenged what I thought, argued with my concepts and ideas, and refused to let me write anything that I did not believe. Without her, there would not have been a book.

Second, there are my secretaries, Hattie Pearl Decell and Mary Lynn Still, who did the typing. Without them, this book would never have gotten to the publisher.

I owe a tremendous debt to my son, Rob, who drew the sketches for the book. These drawings indicate that he is more than a sketch artist. He has unusual insight into imaging the Scripture. Much of this he gained while experiencing the "fifth gospel" firsthand in the Middle East in 1987. His work has been an inspiration to his dad.

I also must thank my nephews, Dr. William B. Morgan, Jr. and Dr. Michael M. Stewart, two outstanding young United Methodist pastors in North Alabama. They have edited what I have written and helped me rewrite portions, enabling me to discover better ways to express myself.

Finally, I want to thank the United Methodists of Mississippi, who support me with their prayers and shared ministry. They have *made him known* to me in many ways. And thanks to the United Methodist congregations in Alabama who nurtured me through my ministry: Wesley Chapel in Sylacauga; Epworth in Huntsville; and Forest Lake in Tuscaloosa. A special thanks goes to my last congregation, Vestavia Hills United Methodist Church in Birmingham, who for more than ten years allowed me the joy of being their pastor and to whom the basic content of this book was first preached. "I thank my God for you whenever I think of you" (Philippians 1:3 Phillips).

Robert C. Morgan
Jackson, Mississippi

Foreword

Someone has facetiously remarked that when Adam and Eve were driven out of the Garden, Adam put his arm around Eve as he attempted to console her with these words: "My dear, we live in an age of transition." Every age from that time to this has been an age of transition. God is constantly changing things. There appear on the horizon new names, new faces, and new ideas.

Practically every denomination is in an age of transition. The writers who helped train my generation, like Fosdick and Tittle and Chappell and many others, have gone on to God's house, but in their places have come new voices in the wilderness; and they are a part of the transition. To me, none is more significant in the transition occurring in The United Methodist Church than Bishop Robert C. Morgan of Mississippi.

Although this is Bishop Morgan's first book, I would not be in error to say that it takes its place in the significant books this new generation has given to the church. As we read these pages, the gospel comes alive; but, more than that, the "fifth gospel"—which we see and feel as it captures us but which can't be written—emerges. What Jesus said and did in these scriptural accounts causes us to discover a new understanding of sin, the sinner, and the Savior. We are reminded that to be a Christian is to be an agent of love.

Bishop Morgan reminds us that bread was Jesus' symbol. He uses bread to talk about mercy and forgiveness as our Lord talked about it: when the prodigal came home, they killed the fatted calf and broke bread together. He uses bread to talk about justice: bread for the physical body and bread for the spiritual body. Jesus said that he was the Bread of Life. In the breaking of bread, Jesus was made known to his disciples.

Bishop Morgan also writes about priorities and the importance of putting first things first. He reminds us of the tension between two expressions of faith—good works and personal commitment. He reminds us that, for better or worse, we are now members of the body of Christ and are the instruments God has chosen to spread his Word and his Kingdom. He reminds us that we must work to create a society where poverty and hunger and racism no longer exist. He challenges us to become change agents in our communities. And he does so using personal illustrations that are dear to him and that become dear to us.

Surely we live in an age of transition. Old things will be made new, and I celebrate that. I thank God for this new generation of young preachers and prophets who stand in the Lord's place and say the Lord's words and count it the high privilege of their life to preach the unsearchable riches of Jesus Christ.

Bishop Morgan's research and scholarship have excited those of us who know him. I recommend this book to you, and I heartily recommend its author.

W. Kenneth Goodson

Bishop of The United Methodist Church
Duke University
Durham, North Carolina

1

Made Known in the Breaking of Bread

The NATURE of God Made Known

KNOWN IN THE BREAKING OF BREAD

*N*ow on that same day two of them were going to a village called *Emmaus, about seven miles from Jerusalem, and talking with each other about all these things that had happened. While they were talking and discussing, Jesus himself came near and went with them, but their eyes were kept from recognizing him. And he said to them, "What are you discussing with each other while you walk along?" They stood still, looking sad. Then one of them, whose name was Cleopas, answered him, "Are you the only stranger in Jerusalem who does not know the things that have taken place there in these days?" He asked them, "What things?" They replied, "The things about Jesus of Nazareth, who was a prophet mighty in deed and word before God and all the people, and how our chief priests and leaders handed him over to be condemned to death and crucified him. But we had hoped that he was the one to redeem Israel. Yes, and besides all this, it is now the third day since these things took place. Moreover, some women of our group astounded us. They were at the tomb early this morning, and when they did not find his body there, they came back and told us that they had indeed seen a vision of angels who said that he was alive. Some of those who were with us went to the tomb and found it just as the women had said; but they did not see him." Then he said to them, "Oh, how foolish you are, and how slow of heart to believe all that the prophets have declared! Was it not necessary that the Messiah should suffer these things and then enter into his glory?" Then beginning with Moses and all the prophets, he interpreted to them the things about himself in the scriptures.*

As they came near the village to which they were going he walked ahead as if he were going on. But they urged him strongly, saying, "Stay with us, because it is almost evening and the day is now nearly over." So he went in to stay with them. When he was at the table with them, he took bread, blessed and broke it, and gave it to them. Then their eyes were opened, and they recognized him; and he vanished from their sight. They said to each other, "Were not our hearts burning within us while he was talking to us on the road, while he was opening the scriptures to us?" That same hour they got up and returned to Jerusalem; and they found the eleven and their companions gathered together. They were saying, "The Lord has risen indeed, and he has appeared to Simon!" Then they told what had happened on the road, and how he had been made known to them in the breaking of bread. (Luke 24:13-35 NRSV)

There are many occasions recorded in the four Gospels when Jesus shared a meal with others. Luke records more of these occasions than any other. This is no accident. Luke was a Gentile. He understood more than anyone the plight of being shut out and rejected. He was cut off from elements of Judaism. He desired a place among "the chosen." In addition, he was a physician, and his compassion for human beings comes out in his interpretation of Jesus as the "one for others." Luke portrays Jesus as being a friend of sinners—one who, without hesitation, sat at the meal table with them and ate and drank with all who invited him. He couldn't have cared less whether they were contemptuous tax collectors or a person the religious community might label "sinner." Jesus' hospitality and acceptance, as well as his indifference to social and religious barriers, endeared him to Luke.

Luke is the only Gospel writer to share the account of the disciples encountering Jesus on the Emmaus Road. In addition to the Emmaus account, there is the appearance in the Upper Room in Jerusalem as recorded in Luke 24:36-48. A third is recorded in Acts 1:1-11, just before the Ascension. In each of the post-Resurrection appearances, Jesus shares in a meal.

Even in his post-Resurrection accounts, Luke recapitulates with his mealtime theme. His method is much like that of a great symphony when the composer reintroduces variations of the same theme throughout the composition.

Sharing a meal and breaking bread was common for Jesus and the disciples. As such, it should not be difficult to understand his disciples recognizing him in the breaking of bread. This is the point of Luke's account of the events on the road and at the table in Emmaus.

Some of the fondest memories from my childhood are those moments with family and friends at mealtime. At least one meal each day was spent in the company of all the family members. All three meals were shared on some occasions. Everything about the meal was special. My mother was a wonderful cook and the meal was a special gift she shared with her family. She prepared the meal sacramentally, my dad blessed the meal ceremonially, and the family consumed it eagerly.

During my childhood, meals were not merely occasions for consuming food and drink; they were also expressions of communion with other family members. It was a time to share your stories and to listen to others share theirs. The table was a classroom. My parents took the opportunity to share insights and impart values. The meal was an occasion when we knew we were loved and accepted. The family table was the scene where broken relations were reconciled and hurts were healed.

I never gave much attention to the number of significant events in the life of Jesus that took place around the supper table until one day a teenager asked me why the Lord's supper was known as the Last Supper. My answer was that it was our Lord's final meal with his disciples before his death. I asked her what she thought, and she replied, "I believe that it was called the Last Supper by the Gospel writer because it was the last of several 'supper events' in the life of Jesus."

This insight from a fifteen year old changed the direction of our Bible study for the following weeks. Together, we outlined the stories in the life of Jesus that took place at mealtime. We counted over twenty occasions when Jesus actually participated in a meal or shared a parable related to a mealtime experience. In a number of instances, the narrative seems to imply he shared a meal while he was a guest in someone's home.

Jesus' method of teaching was to use every opportunity at his disposal to communicate his message. He focused on the obvious to make his point to those who followed him. Mealtime provided Jesus with the platform to make known his teachings on matters such as forgiveness, salvation, humility, servanthood, justice, and life.

To fully understand the significance of these meals, we need to understand the role of "the meal" and the symbol of "bread" among the people of Jesus' time and among the people of the Middle East today. Bread plays a significant role in the imagery of the New Testament. *Bethlehem*, the birthplace of Jesus, means "house of bread." It should be of little surprise that Jesus was recognized or made known in the act of breaking bread. After all, he was the one who claimed, "I am the bread of life" (John 6:35 NRSV). For the people who heard Jesus make this claim, bread served at least three functions.

First, bread was the *staple* of life. The diet of most Jews during Jesus' day was barley bread and olives. Fish was added to the diet if you lived near the sea. Bread, however, was the primary food source. This was especially true for the poor, which included 90 percent of the people during Jesus' earthly ministry. They could not exist without it.

Second, bread was the *symbol* of God's good gift of life and God's gift of the seed and the harvest of grain. Therefore, the people had tremendous respect for bread. Because of this reverence for bread, one never cut bread with a knife. One broke the bread with respect, grateful for God's gift of the bounty of the land. Bread was never thrown in the garbage. When bread was hard and inedible it was soaked in water and fed to birds. Bread was never wasted or discarded.

Understanding bread as the symbol of life and sustenance, the Bible reader can more readily grasp the magnitude of Jesus' statement, "I am the bread of life. Whoever comes to me will never be hungry." The people to whom Jesus spoke knew that they could not live without bread—their daily sustenance. Jesus was saying to

18

them, "What bread is for the physical body, I am for your hungry hearts; I alone can satisfy your hunger; I am more than you need."

The third function of bread, and one of the most important functions as it relates to this book, was that it was a *sacrament* of life. It was used as a covenant. There are a number of covenant ceremonies in the Bible, but the breaking of bread or the shared bread seems to be the most prominent. The covenant of bread is used throughout the patriarchal stories in Genesis as an act of reconciliation, such as the story of Jacob and Laban (Genesis 29:31).

When persons experienced separation or alienation and were reconciled, they shared bread together to symbolize their reconciliation. Because of the sacredness of meals, the people of faith saw meals and food as appropriate ways of being with God and celebrating the mystery of his presence.

The Last Supper is what most Christians think of as an example of a sacred meal. However, any meal might be used to ratify covenants in Jesus' time.

There are numerous accounts in the gospel narrative where Jesus was portrayed as dining with persons from all walks of life. He was criticized more for eating with publicans and sinners than for anything else he did. What bothered the Pharisees and Scribes was that by eating with the sinners, Jesus offered forgiveness and reconciliation to the outcasts of society. But because Jesus would not discriminate when he broke bread with others, the meal table or the banquet room became one of the primary arenas where Jesus disclosed the true nature of God to the world.

Important persons were eager to have Jesus dine with them, so they extended invitations to him. On at least one occasion we know of, Jesus invited himself to dinner with Zacchaeus. Jesus also customarily broke bread with his disciples at the close of the day. At these repasts, Jesus conversed freely with his companions, and on these occasions, more than any others, they came near to him and learned to know him. Jesus took the occasion of breaking bread to make known the most important things we understand about God.

As we study a few of these mealtime encounters, it is important for us to remember the significance of the meal and the function of bread in biblical times as the staple of life, as a symbol of life, and as a sacrament of life.

My purpose in these pages will be to address those aspects in Jesus' life and ministry that were made known while "breaking bread" with sinners, publicans, friends, disciples, Pharisees, and the host of others he encountered at mealtime. I will attempt to incorporate what I have discovered from the "fifth gospel" to help you better understand what Jesus made known in the breaking of bread. At the same time, I will share my personal reflection on the meals of Jesus and the reconciling encounters I experienced while "breaking bread" with others. My wish is that some new insight about Jesus will be *made known* to you.

2
Look Who's Coming to Dinner!

SALVATION Made Known

TAX COLLECTORS COME TO THE TABLE

*A*fter this he went out and saw a tax collector named Levi, sitting at the tax booth; and he said to him, "Follow me." And he got up, left everything, and followed him.

Then Levi gave a great banquet for him in his house; and there was a large crowd of tax collectors and others sitting at the table with them. The Pharisees and their scribes were complaining to his disciples, saying, "Why do you eat and drink with tax collectors and sinners?" Jesus answered, "Those who are well have no need of a physician, but those who are sick; I have come to call not the righteous but sinners to repentance."

Then they said to him, "John's disciples, like the disciples of the Pharisees, frequently fast and pray, but your disciples eat and drink." Jesus said to them, "You cannot make wedding guests fast while the bridegroom is with them, can you? The days will come when the bridegroom will be taken away from them, and then they will fast in those days."

He entered Jericho and was passing through it. A man was there named Zacchaeus; he was a chief tax collector and was rich. He was trying to see who Jesus was, but on account of the crowd he could not, because he was short in stature. So he ran ahead and climbed a sycamore tree to see him, because he was going to pass that way. When Jesus came to the place, he looked up and said to him, "Zacchaeus, hurry and come down; for I must stay at your house today." So he hurried down and was happy to welcome him. All who saw it began to grumble and said, "He has gone to be the guest of one who is a sinner." Zacchaeus stood there and said to the Lord, "Look, half of my possessions, Lord, I will give to the poor; and if I have defrauded anyone of anything, I will pay back four times as much." Then Jesus said to him, "Today salvation has come to this house, because he too is a son of Abraham. For the Son of Man came to seek out and to save the lost." (Luke 5:27-35; 19:1-10 NRSV)

I have a dear friend who is in the salvage business. He has been very successful at taking the old and discarded and reclaiming it.

One of the many charms of Holland is that it is a country built largely by the process of salvaging. Much of Holland is land that the Dutch have slowly reclaimed by pushing back the sea.

All around us we experience a renewed emphasis on reclaiming our streams and rivers, as well as the air we breathe. We want to recycle precious materials that we have thoughtlessly thrown out over the years. This interest should be commended, and we all must join the fight.

How strange it is that while we engage in such a fight, we allow our most precious and most irreplaceable resource—human beings—to be junked. What would happen if we took all the social rejects—the people whom we have discarded—and recycled them just as we seek to do with aluminum cans and glass bottles? This idea is not so new or radical as it may sound; this is what Jesus did.

The practice of never giving up on people needs to be the agenda of the church. An example of this happened in a local church I served. A bank executive who was an active member of the church was arrested and imprisoned for misuse of funds. On the day prior to his arrest, he came to my office and confessed what he had done. He was filled with remorse and shame, not only because he feared being caught but because he dreaded the embarrassment that would come to his family, friends, and church. He knew that what he had done was wrong, and for this he was truly repentant.

The congregation ministered to this man and his family in a wonderful way. He was imprisoned in a federal correction center in the state where he lived. Each week, two or three men in the congregation would drive to the prison and visit with him. Different men would go on alternating weeks. I accompanied them on a number of occasions. They did this each week he was incarcerated.

When he was released, several of these men went to the prison with his wife to meet him. Then they drove to the church and met me in the

24

chapel. The other men who had been so faithful and supportive joined us as we celebrated the sacrament of Holy Communion.

Jesus made it known early in his earthly ministry that he would seek to reclaim the lost and forgotten. The first meal that Luke recorded of Jesus sharing bread with others is recorded in the fifth chapter of Luke. The meal takes place in the home of Levi, a tax collector—a social and religious outcast. Levi is known to us as Matthew. The most startling aspect of this account by Luke is that Jesus invites someone like Matthew into the company of his disciples. Equally startling is that Matthew eagerly accepts the invitation.

Luke intended for his readers to understand that Jesus' ministry was not to "those who are well and need no physician, but to those who are sick . . . to call not the righteous, but the sinners to repentance" (5:31, 32 NRSV). This particular account comes on the heels of Jesus' visit to his hometown, Nazareth, where he addressed the local synagogue, declaring that Isaiah's words were to be fulfilled in his life and ministry.

> The Spirit of the Lord is upon me,
> Because he anointed me to preach good tidings to the poor:
> He hath sent me to proclaim release to the captives,
> And recovering of sight to the blind,
> To set at liberty them that are bruised. (Luke 4:18 Phillips)

From the foundation of Jesus' earthly ministry in both Nazareth and Capernaum, he made it known that he would identify with the least and lowly of humankind.

This sounds appropriate and simple in the context of the pages of Scripture, yet we fail to realize the mandate of our Lord who calls us to do likewise. Unfortunately, there are good and well-intentioned religious people who openly justify standing apart from those who need acceptance and love and forgiveness, and who defend their separation in the name of purity. Jacob Neusner, in *From Politics to Piety: The Emergence of Pharisaic Judaism,* refers to Pharisaism as an expression of that separatist impulse, noting that one mark of religious demagoguery is to quote Scripture out of context, using Scripture phrases such as, "Come ye apart. Be ye separate. Don't associate with dogs, nor cast your pearls before swine. Minister to your own kind. Forget about those sinners. They deserve what they get."

An old preacher was addicted to alcohol. He would do all right for a while, and then he would stumble. When he stumbled, he lost favor with everyone: his family, church, and bishop. When he was sober, he was a very pious and judgmental brother. But there was one person, a young pastor, who always came to him when he was in trouble. This pastor had the reputation of never giving up on anyone.

After many years of second chances, the old preacher began to drink again. This time he was forced to surrender his ordination credentials. The young pastor did not hear about it for several days. When he did, he remembered that the old preacher had a little family farm where he would normally take refuge. So the young pastor drove the distance and after some searching found the little farm. He was greeted at the door by a grateful wife. She told him that the old preacher saw him driving up and was hiding behind the barn. The young pastor walked out to him and found him huddled in a corner.

"Damn you," the old preacher said, "I can't stand you, but I knew you would be the only one to come. Thank God, you never let me go." What a wonderful reputation to have, to be known as the one who will come to the aid of the forgotten!

The Pharisees and their scribes criticized Jesus not because Jesus invited Matthew to be a disciple, but because he ate with him. "Why do you eat and drink with tax collectors and sinners?" (Luke 5:30 NRSV).

The meal that the religious leaders referred to was the feast that Matthew gave in honor of Jesus after Matthew "left all" to follow Jesus. He invited his associates and friends to share his good news. The friends of Matthew were the sinners to whom the Pharisees referred. Among them were other publicans who in the eyes of Jews were the most contemptible and despised of society. They were no better than thieves and murderers.

Luke records a similar experience later in his Gospel account: the story of Zacchaeus of Jericho. Jesus was on his last journey to Jerusalem. He and his disciples were moving toward that inevitable conflict that would lead to the Crucifixion. They came to Jericho and were greeted by a throng of people who had heard of Jesus. Word of his coming had spread through Jericho, so Zacchaeus, a tax collector, had heard of his arrival.

Like Matthew, or any other tax collector, Zacchaeus was a hated man. He had purchased from Rome the tax collecting concession, which had made him a wealthy man. The tax collector was not only the collector of taxes but also the assessor of taxes. To acquire this lucrative position he had to pay a high price to the Roman government. When taxes were assessed, the tax collector was at liberty to set them as high as he wished. All that he could make above what he had paid the Romans was profit.

This is why both Matthew and Zacchaeus were considered outcasts by their own people. They were regarded as persons who had sold out to the enemy in return for material wealth. For this reason they were shunned completely.

Luke describes Zacchaeus as a short man, and for that reason he climbed a sycamore tree to assure himself of a glimpse of the Master as he passed by. More than likely he hoped no one would spot him in such an undignified perch. But Jesus stopped under the tree and looked up to call him by name and issue his invitation. No one was more stunned than Zacchaeus that he of all people would be selected for the honor of entertaining the visiting rabbi and his disciples.

The people of Jericho gasped at the words of Jesus and murmured that he was going to be the guest of a known sinner. Jesus passed up any opportunity to be the guest of the religious leadership of the city, who might have welcomed the conversation of the visiting rabbi. He did not think to take a close look at some of the faithful and pious Pharisees, who would have been honored to be singled out to be

Jesus' host. Instead, he picked a sinner and symbolically answered, once and for all, the question that every Pharisee and scribe raised about his association with the sinners and outcasts. Jesus made known with his actions that God is never beyond visiting his children. They are all his who "make haste to come down" and receive him into their homes and hearts.

It is apparent that both Matthew and Zacchaeus had heard of Jesus. His reputation preceded him. This is evidenced by the fact that when Jesus called, Matthew immediately left his "tax table" and "left everything behind." Zacchaeus also must have known of Jesus to let his curiosity carry him so far. It was no small decision to run the risks of a scornful crowd by climbing the tree to see Jesus.

When Matthew stepped out from behind the table and Zacchaeus climbed down from the tree into the presence of Jesus, they saw themselves for what they had become. Although Luke goes to greater length to portray the character of Zacchaeus than he does of Matthew, their similarities cannot be ignored. Both of them were greedy for wealth and were willing to sacrifice friendship and acceptance by their communities to have it. For them, money was the greatest value, and they were sure that it would bring them the only happiness they needed. They sacrificed the dignity of character, integrity, and position in the religious community to get "the stuff" of life. Obviously peace of mind and self-respect had eluded both of these men.

So when they looked up into the eyes of the Master, their shabby character and their drab, friendless existence showed the kind of persons they had become. You dare not look into the eyes of Jesus if you are unwilling to be honest in seeing yourself for who you are. Jesus looked at persons without accusation, but to see him was to stand self-accused. So it was with Matthew and Zacchaeus.

Jesus made it known to all that he came to seek and save sinners and to "recycle" them. In this case, as in so many others, he reclaimed them over a meal.

3

The World's Most Famous Barbecue

FORGIVENESS Made Known

THE STAY-AT-HOME STAYS OUT

*T*hen Jesus said, "There was a man who had two sons. The younger of them said to his father, 'Father, give me the share of the property that will belong to me.' So he divided his property between them. A few days later the younger son gathered all he had and traveled to a distant country, and there he squandered his property in dissolute living. When he had spent everything, a severe famine took place throughout that country, and he began to be in need. So he went and hired himself out to one of the citizens of that country, who sent him to his fields to feed the pigs. He would gladly have filled himself with the pods that the pigs were eating; and no one gave him anything. But when he came to himself he said, 'How many of my father's hired hands have bread enough and to spare, but here I am dying of hunger! I will get up and go to my father, and I will say to him, "Father, I have sinned against heaven and before you; I am no longer worthy to be called your son; treat me like one of your hired hands."' So he set off and went to his father. But while he was still far off, his father saw him and was filled with compassion; he ran and put his arms around him and kissed him. Then the son said to him. 'Father, I have sinned against heaven and before you; I am no longer worthy to be called your son.' But the father said to his slaves, 'Quickly, bring out a robe—the best one—and put it on him; put a ring on his finger and sandals on his feet. And get the fatted calf and kill it, and let us eat and celebrate; for this son of mine was dead and is alive again; he was lost and is found!' And they began to celebrate.

"Now his elder son was in the field; and when he came and approached the house, he heard music and dancing. He called one of the slaves and asked what was going on. He replied, 'Your brother has come, and your father has killed the fatted calf, because he has got him back safe and sound.' Then he became angry and refused to go in. His father came out and began to plead with him. But he answered his father, 'Listen! For all these

31

years I have been working like a slave for you, and I have never disobeyed your command; yet you have never given me even a young goat so that I might celebrate with my friends. But when this son of yours came back, who has devoured your property with prostitutes, you killed the fatted calf for him!' Then the father said to him, 'Son, you are always with me, and all that is mine is yours. But we had to celebrate and rejoice, because this brother of yours was dead and has come to life; he was lost and has been found.' "
(Luke 15:11-24 NRSV)

When Jesus states, "I am the bread of life," he is saying in essence, "I am the one who can help you bring reconciliation in your broken relationships, and I bring forgiveness and reconciliation with God." The very fact that Jesus eats with tax collectors and sinners is an act of forgiveness and reconciliation. The Pharisees were enraged by this gesture. Hence their repeated criticism, "He eats with tax collectors and sinners."

The setting for the entire fifteenth chapter of the Gospel according to Luke could have been a meal. The chapter begins with the statement that the tax collectors and sinners were all drawing near to listen to Jesus. The Pharisees and the scribes were grumbling and saying, "This fellow welcomes sinners and eats with them" (Luke 15:2 NRSV). This was the preface for Jesus' parables of the lost sheep, the lost coins, and the prodigal son.

Jesus and the disciples were in the region of Perea, which is located on the eastern side of the Jordan River. They were en route from Galilee to Jerusalem. It was here that Jesus shared one of his most well known and beloved parables, the story of the prodigal son.

It is a story of a rebellious son who wearies of the duties and responsibilities of home and family. He requests and is granted his portion of the family fortune and journeys into the "far country." Some time later, after he has wasted his inheritance, he realizes the mistake he has made and he longs for his father's house.

There were several things that the prodigal son was prepared to say to his father when he returned home. He thought about it long and hard while he was in the distant country. In fact, he rehearsed his "coming-home" speech. He said to himself, "I will say to him, 'I have sinned against heaven and against you . . . I am no longer worthy to be called your son . . . make me as one of your hired hands or servants.' "

With his speech in mind, he headed for home. The parable states that while the son was still far off, his father saw him and was filled with compassion. The father ran to meet him and put his arms around him and kissed him. The father's welcome was in plain view of all the neighbors and hired hands.

After the father had greeted him, the returning son began his litany. "Father, I have sinned against heaven and before you; I am no longer worthy to be called your son." But before the son could finish his speech by saying . . . "make me as one of your servants," the father interrupted him and refused to let him finish.

The father countered with four actions. First he said to his servants, "Quickly, bring out a robe . . . the best . . . and put it on him." Hired hands or servants wore simple tunics so they could stoop in the fields; sons wore robes, and his father wanted everyone to know this was his son. Second, the father said . . . "put a ring on his finger." This is not just any ring, but the family crest signifying to all the son's restoration to the family. Third, he ordered the servants to "put sandals on his feet." Servants went barefooted; sons wore sandals. Finally, he did the most symbolic thing he could do to let everyone know his son was restored and forgiven. He ordered the servants to "get the fatted calf and kill it, and let us eat and celebrate. For this son of mine was dead and is alive again; he was lost and is found." And they began to celebrate. It was a celebration of forgiveness and reconciliation.

The South is known for wonderful barbecue restaurants. I have eaten in many of them. They all have at least two things in common. They all serve good food, and they all have the same slogan, "The World's Most Famous Barbecue." But the barbecue prepared for the prodigal son is really the most "famous" of all time.

When the father desired to demonstrate his forgiveness for his son and to make that fact known to the runaway son and to all his neighbors in the little town, he prepared a banquet. He called on the servants to kill the fatted calf, which was reserved for special occasions, and to prepare the banquet. He invited everyone in the village to the meal to let them know that his son was forgiven and restored to the family.

Realizing that the reconciliation meal was truly a gesture of forgiveness and acceptance, we can better understand the behavior of the older brother. He refused to come in to the celebration supper because he did not forgive. Mealtime is a forgiving time. Since he did not forgive his younger brother he remained on the outside, sulking.

The older son refused to come in even after the bidding of his father. He said, "All these years I have slaved for you, and you never even offered me a skinny goat, but when this rascal son of yours comes home, you kill the fatted calf and celebrate with all the neighbors."

There are two lost sons in the story. Bishop Gerald Kennedy called them the son who *stayed* and the son who *strayed*. In this wonderful and familiar story Jesus *made known* the forgiving nature of the heavenly Father. He is saying that all prodigals, those who have strayed and those who have stayed, are welcome home and the invitation is always open. Regardless of what you have done or how far you have strayed into the distant country, the waiting, loving Father will welcome you to the table of forgiveness and offer you the bread of reconciliation.

In most of the post-Resurrection appearances of Jesus, he ate with his disciples or asked if there was food. Just prior to and after the Crucifixion, the disciples had abandoned him, and it was in the breaking of bread that he *made known* his forgiving spirit.

One of the most notable examples is recorded at the end of John's Gospel. Jesus met the disciples on the shores of the Sea of Galilee early one morning after a night when the disciples had been fishing. He called to them from the shore, and they came in for a breakfast that he had prepared for them.

Imagine what must have been going through the minds of the disciples as they gathered around the breakfast fire. Simon Peter had denied Jesus three times after he had vowed to follow him to death. All the others had fled for their lives in fear and had hid behind locked doors. Then, following the Crucifixion, they had returned to their former fishing trade in the Sea of Galilee. This meal scene was an occasion where Jesus recalled all of them to follow him. But before he called them again he said, "I will prepare your breakfast . . . a meal. This is my way of saying it is all right. . . . You are forgiven . . . follow me . . . come on back. I know that you feel awful. You are hurt and embarrassed, but you are forgiven. Come share this reconciling meal with me and go out from here to do what I command you to do." Simon Peter denied knowing Jesus three times, but after the meal of reconciliation on the Galilean shore, he vowed his love for Christ three times.

Other post-Resurrection appearances included the breaking of bread. Jesus shared a meal with the two disciples at Emmaus (Luke 24:31). Luke records that Jesus appeared to the disciples in Jerusalem and while they "disbelieved for joy," Jesus said to them, "Have you anything here to eat?" (Luke 24:41). He wanted to demonstrate his forgiveness in spite of their unfaithfulness. The same gesture is true when Luke records in Acts 1:4, "while he was eating a meal with them." Mark records that Jesus appeared to them "as they were sitting at table" (Mark 16:14). In the book of Revelation the Lord says, "Here I stand knocking at the door; if anyone hears my voice and opens the door, I will come in and sit down to supper with him and he with me" (Revelation 3:20 NEB). In other words, the invitation to the table is for anyone who will open the door.

What Jesus said and did in these scriptural accounts causes one to discover a new understanding regarding sin, the sinner, and the savior.

These wonderful stories cause us to rethink Jesus' measure of sin. His listening audience for the story of the loving father and his two sons included not only his own disciples and the residents of the Perea, but also those Pharisees and scribes who followed him from place to place monitoring his every word. The listeners were amazed that Jesus portrayed the waiting father as one who stressed forgiveness rather than the sin of the rebellious son.

It was the older brother, not the father, who was quick to point out the terrible things the younger son had done. He said that his younger brother had "spent all of his money on prostitutes" (vs. 30), but Jesus did not say anything about prostitutes in his story. It was the conclusion of the judgmental older brother that this was what his younger brother did. Similar to most cases of judgment, this conclusion may say more about the older brother than the repentant younger son.

Jesus' attitude toward sin, as made known in this story, is not unlike the story of the woman brought to Jesus by the Pharisees and scribes recorded in John. She had been caught in the act of adultery, and making her stand before all of them, they asked Jesus what they should do. They reminded him that the law of Moses commanded the stoning of such a woman. Jesus bent down and wrote with his finger on the ground. While doing this he said, "Let anyone among you who is without sin be the first to throw a stone at her." John wrote that they all went away. Jesus straightened up and said, "Woman, where are they? Has no one condemned you?" She replied, "No one, sir." And Jesus said, "Neither do I condemn you. Go your way, and from now on do not sin again."

One cannot help comparing the language the older brother and the Pharisees used regarding sin to that of the forgiving father and Jesus. We also should compare what Jesus said to the woman accused of adultery to the words he had for the Pharisees: "Woe to you, scribes and Pharisees, hypocrites! For you tithe mint, dill, and cumin, and have neglected the weightier matters of the law: justice and mercy and faith. It is these that you ought to have practiced without neglecting the others. You blind guides! You strain out at a gnat but swallow a camel" (Matthew 23:23-24 NRSV). Jesus was not making light of adultery or conduct similar to that of the rebellious son. He certainly must have taken a grave view of such behavior. Rather, Jesus seemed to be implying that while adultery and rebelliousness are wrong, they are no worse than the sins of hypocrisy, pride, and self-righteousness. When you examine the scathing description Jesus gave for the behavior of the scribes and Pharisees, it is difficult not to conclude that in his opinion, theirs were worse sins.

There were two old citizens talking. "I guess I'll go to heaven," said one to the other. "I never drank liquor, gambled, or ran around on my wife."

"That's right," said the other. "You never drank, gambled, or ran around on your wife. But you sure kept up with and talked about everyone you knew who did."

Jesus forces us to reexamine our understanding of sin. If we are audacious enough to set ourselves as judges of any one, we do so at our own peril.

In the light of this marvelous story in the Gospel according to Luke, Jesus also causes us to take a new look at the sinner. The Pharisees believed in forgiveness and encouraged repentance, but they usually expected one to perform some act of repentance to demonstrate the change. Jesus, on the other hand, seemed to accept people before they made any promise to change. There are those who say, "Repent and be saved." Jesus declares that God's love is better than that! God forgives you, and because of his forgiveness and love, you repent.

Parents hearing Jesus tell of a father and a rebellious son could easily identify. They knew firsthand what it meant to have their sons rebel and embarrass them before their neighbors. It was the common practice to disown such children. What a surprise it must have been to hear Jesus' story. If the truth were known, the behavior of the older brother was more in keeping with their understanding of how you dealt with a sinner. They would agree that the elder brother was justified in not sitting down to the reconciliation meal with the returning younger brother. They were stunned by Jesus' story of the father's forgiving spirit.

There was a rabbinical tale at the time of Jesus that was popular among the people. Most everyone in Jesus' audience would have known the story. It was about a king who had a rebellious son. He left home and behaved in much the same way that the prodigal son did in

Jesus' story. However, in the rabbinical story the son returns and the "gracious king" allows the son to return as a servant. The rabbis pointed out the generosity of the king. Jesus, on the other hand, was anxious to make known that God is better than that. He said the prodigal was restored to "full relationship"—a much different way to treat the sinner.

The scribes and Pharisees wanted to stone the woman accused of adultery, but Jesus refused to condemn her. He forgave her and set her free with the admonition to sin no more. He set her free so that she might live and be a blessing to her family and others, rather than a curse.

One of professional football's greatest players tells of the occasion when he was arrested by the police for indecent exposure. He spent time in counseling and rehabilitation for several weeks before returning to his team.

When he returned, he joined the team for the weekly game review and team meeting. He asked his coach for an opportunity to speak to the team. He expressed his regret in having embarrassed them. He begged for their forgiveness. There was not much response when he completed his remarks and sat down. The lights were turned off and the projector was turned on so that the team could review Sunday's game.

Silence was broken in the room by players clearing their throats or moving chairs. Out of the darkened room, one by one, team members came over and placed their hand on his shoulder or took his hand. They said things like "welcome back," "we are with you," "you will make it," and returned to their seats in silence.

The player said that one of the big defensive ends came over and whispered in his ear . . . "Forgiven, forgotten, forever!" He said it was the first time he understood what it meant to be a forgiven and restored person.

What Jesus reveals to us about forgiveness demands that we rethink our understanding of sin and the sinner. When we do, we realize more than ever our need for the savior.

As the Epistle to the Hebrew Christians puts it, we have for our Savior not a "high priest who is unable to sympathize with our weaknesses, but one who in every respect has been tested as we are, yet without sin" (Hebrews 4:14 NRSV). In other words, our Lord knows the sickness of the human heart. He knows about loneliness and love, about temptation and turmoil, about sorrow and suffering. He has been there, and he is far more forgiving of us than we are of ourselves.

When we take a close look at the relationship between the father and his rebellious son, we see what a wonderful savior God is. We see the way God sees through the eyes of the father. We see the infinite joy that the father has in the son's return. We see how, for his son's sake, he is unwilling to condemn, believing in human nature, seeing the potential, offering another chance, and having all the hope therein. We sense the joy in the heart of the father as he calls for a special celebration meal to commemorate the son's return and total acceptance.

> Amazing Grace!
> How sweet the sound
> that saved a wretch like me!
> I once was lost,
> but now am found;
> was blind, but now I see.

A young doctor was assigned to be in charge of a hospital located in the slums of London. He had not been there long when a boy about six years of age was brought in who had a severe case of diphtheria. The boy was even then gasping and choking, and in a matter of moments, his life would be gone. Even though he had never performed such an operation, the young doctor knew that only emergency surgery could save the child. So he performed a tracheotomy, an incision in the windpipe. He was assisted by a bright young nurse who had received her degree in nursing only a short time before. With fear and trembling, he inserted a tube in the incision and the young boy began to breathe without difficulty.

In the early hours of the morning, the doctor heard a loud pounding on his door. Opening it, he found the young nurse who had helped him. Her job entailed sitting up through the long night to make certain the tube for breathing remained open. But though her spirit was willing, her flesh was weak; she, too, was exhausted from the strain of surgery. She had fallen asleep, and while she was asleep, the tube became blocked and the boy had died.

At this point, the doctor lost his head and swore that she would be reported and punished for this. After a while, he called her into his office and read the report to her while she stood there trembling with fear, overcome with remorse and shame. When he had finished he said, "Well, have you anything to say?" She bowed her head and dared to look up and turned her tear-splashed face toward him. "Please, sir," she said falteringly, "give me another chance."

It had not occurred to the doctor that he might do this. It was all cut and dried, so far as he was concerned. She had failed. Her mistake had cost a life. She must pay. It was just that simple. He could not sleep that night. He kept hearing her cry, "Please give me another chance." All night he wrestled with the memory of that voice, and the Lord tormented him with reminders of mercy and compassion. The next morning he tore up the report and called her in and explained to her that all was forgiven.

Years later, that young nurse went on to become one of England's great nurses and the head of one of the country's largest children's hospitals. She was loved by all, giving herself over and over again to children who needed her love and great heart. Suppose she had fled and not faced up to the wrong that was in her action? Suppose the doctor had not given her another chance? The world is a better place because he did.

Jesus makes it known that God will not do less. The God of Jesus is a God of the second chance. That is why he prepares the fatted calf for the banquet of forgiveness for all who return home. He is a merciful God—the God of beginning again.

What a savior! He knows who we are and loves us so much that he died for us so that we might have second chances, new starts, and other days. He invites us to the table of forgiveness.

4
Serving People and Tables

SERVANTHOOD Made Known

TAKING THE FORM OF A SERVANT

*N*ow before the festival of the Passover, Jesus knew that his hour had come to depart from this world and go to the Father. Having loved his own who were in the world, he loved them to the end. The devil had already put it into the heart of Judas son of Simon Iscariot to betray him. And during supper Jesus, knowing that the Father had given all things into his hands, and that he had come from God and was going to God, got up from the table, took off his outer robe, and tied a towel around himself. Then he poured water into a basin and began to wash the disciples' feet and to wipe them with the towel that was tied around him. He came to Simon Peter, who said to him, "Lord, are you going to wash my feet?" Jesus answered, "You do not know now what I am doing, but later you will understand." Peter said to him, "You will never wash my feet." Jesus answered, "Unless I wash you, you have no share with me." Simon Peter said to him, "Lord, not my feet only but also my hands and my head!" Jesus said to him, "One who has bathed does not need to wash, except for the feet, but is entirely clean. And you are clean, though not all of you." For he knew who was to betray him; for this reason he said, "Not all of you are clean."

After he had washed their feet, had put on his robe, and had returned to the table, he said to them, "Do you know what I have done to you? You call me Teacher and Lord—and you are right, for that is what I am. So if I, your Lord and Teacher, have washed your feet, you also ought to wash one another's feet. For I have set you an example, that you also should do as I have done to you. Very truly, I tell you, servants are not greater than their master, nor are messengers greater than the one who sent them. If you know these things, you are blessed if you do them. (John 13:1-17 NRSV)

It had been a trying week for Jesus in Jerusalem. Many of his closest friends had encouraged him not to travel to the city for the

Passover this year. The crowds were restless, and his disciples had reason for their concern regarding his safety. The religious leaders were plotting against him, and there were rumors of a sinister plot to do away with him. The tension and stress of the days before were beginning to show.

Another factor that fed into the tension of the evening was between the disciples themselves. There were internal concerns about places of leadership and position. There had been hints of this friction on other occasions, but it had become more pronounced in the last few days.

On the way to Jerusalem, the mother of James and John had taken Jesus aside to speak a word on behalf of her sons. "When you come into your kingdom, I want you to remember my boys. They have been with you from the first. They deserve prominent positions. Let one sit on the right, and one on your left." The other disciples were indignant. Harsh words were spoken, and there was division in the camp.

It must have been a sad sight. Jesus walked ahead burdened by what awaited him in Jerusalem, while his disciples argued among themselves. This mood did not leave the group after they arrived in Jerusalem. They were concerned about their own position and benefits in the kingdom.

This is the background leading up to the last meal that Jesus would share with his inner circle of disciples. He knew how strategic the evening would be. One evening remained in which he was to lay a wonderful commission upon the hearts of these men he loved.

Jesus gave careful planning and preparation for the evening. It needed to be a secret place where they would not be disturbed. By this time, Jesus and the disciples were in hiding. They would slip into the city during the day and return to the Mount of Olives area and Bethany for the evening.

The Synoptics give more detail of the preparation than does John. Luke gives the most detailed account:

Jesus sent off Peter and John with the words, "Go and make all the preparations for us to eat the Passover."

"Where would you like for us to do this?" they asked. And he replied, "Listen, just as you are going into the city a man carrying a jug of water will meet you. Follow him to the house he is making for. Then say to the owner of the house, 'The master has this message for you . . . which is the room where my disciples and I may eat the Passover?' And he will take you upstairs and show you a large room furnished for our needs. Make all the preparations there."

So they went off and found everything exactly as he had told them it would be, and they made the Passover preparations. (Luke 22:8-13 Phillips)

It is worth noting that men did not carry water jars. This chore was performed only by women. The man would therefore have been easily identified. It was a prearranged signal. Perhaps Jesus had contacts and hidden disciples of whom many of his closest followers were not aware. James Fleming suggests the man was an Essene monk, living in town.

So many important things were made known on this special night and in this special place. Jesus did something prior to the supper that, in some respects, is the most timely and tender touch in the Bible.

To understand the significance of what happened we need to have a clear image of the setting. The reference in this synoptic gospel passage indicates that the Upper Room was a furnished room. This implies that the room was furnished with three tables joined together in a *U* formation. The tables were low to the floor, enabling the guests to recline on their left elbow and eat with their right hand. Others might choose to sit upright on the floor.

The host or head table was the right wing of the table arrangement. The host's place was second from the end. The places of honor were to the left and right of the host at the head table. The least place of honor was the last position on the left wing.

One of the eastern customs was to wash the feet of the house guests. This chore was normally performed by servants of the host. A pitcher of water, a basin, and towels, along with the servants were provided at the entrance. Sandals, which were the most common shoes of the time, did not provide much protection from the dust of the open road. Some have suggested that since Jesus and the disciples did not have servants, they took turns washing one another's feet. The designated server would normally take the least seat at the table, which was closest to the door.

Look at the scene on this special night. We have already alluded to the tension and diversity among the disciples. They drift into the room one or two at a time, so as not to draw attention to their movements. They enter the furnished Upper Room, tired and dusty at the end of a frustrating week. There is jealousy and discord among them.

Who will volunteer to wash the feet of their fellow disciples? The pitcher of water, the basin, and towels were in their places. Who will agree to serve tonight? James or John? No way, they were moving toward the honored seats. Who? Peter? He had his sights on the honored place. No one moved toward the towel and the basin. No one was willing on this night to humble themselves and wash feet.

One cannot help wondering what Jesus was thinking. He must have agonized over the obstinance of the disciples. Surely he must have had a sinking feeling at the thought of leaving his mission in their hands. He did not say a word. Instead of using words, he rose from his place and walked to the towels, poured water into the basin, and took a towel. Then he moved from disciple to disciple, washing their feet. While he was doing this, not a word was said. The only sound in the room was the sound of an occasional splashing of water.

It must have been an awesome sight for these rebellious disciples. They had heard him teach and preach for the past three years, but they had never experienced so strong a sermon as they saw on this night.

When at last he came to Peter, the silence was broken. Peter being last may indicate that he was occupying the least seat and should have been the one designated to wash the others' feet. Jesus would begin, as custom dictated, at the head table and move around to the least seat, stopping at each place to wash the disciple's feet until he reached Peter.

It has been said of Peter that the only time he opened his mouth was to change feet, or as someone else has said, "Peter belonged to that numerous company of people who, when they don't know what to say, say it anyway."

Peter said to him, "You must never wash my feet!"
Jesus said, "Unless you let me wash you, Peter, . . . you cannot be my true partner."
"Then Lord," returned Simon Peter, "please—not just my feet but my hands and face as well." (John 13:8-9 Phillips)

When Jesus had washed their feet, he sat down again and spoke to them, "Do you understand what I have just done for you? You call me 'teacher' and 'Lord' and you are right, for I am your teacher and your Lord. But if I, your Lord, wash your feet, you must be ready to wash one another's feet. I have done this for you as an example so that you might do as I have done. The son of man came not to be served but to be a servant, that is the only greatness. To be my disciple you must be willing to be a servant to the world."

It is essential to remember that these disciples and everyone living in the world at this time knew what it meant to be ruled by power. Greatness was measured by power and wealth. Jesus said to the disciples, "This is not to be true of you. You must be different. Unless you are different, you will make no difference. I have given you the example. Greatness in my kingdom will be in terms of love and servanthood."

Can you imagine the shock of these disciples? This was not the first time Jesus had said this. Jesus was resolutely calling them to humble themselves as servants and commanded them to love and serve others. This was the way they would achieve greatness. If the truth was known, Judas was not the only Zealot in the crowd. They probably all had latent "power ambition," and they had hoped Jesus would be the one who would give them more power.

Now he speaks of greatness coming from roles they have always associated with the weak and the powerless. Jesus called them to a life of love and service.

Listen to the words of Paul, addressed to the young church at Philippi:

> Let your attitude to life be that of Christ Jesus himself. For he, who had always been God by nature, did not cling to his privileges as God's equal, but stripped himself of every advantage by consenting to be a slave by nature. . . . He humbled himself by living a life of utter obedience, to the point of death, and the death he died was the death of a common criminal. That is why God has now lifted him to the heights, and has given him the name beyond all names, so that at the name of Jesus "every knee shall bow," whether in Heaven or earth or under the earth. And that is why, in the end, "every tongue shall confess" that Jesus Christ is Lord, to the glory of God the Father. (Philippians 2:5-11 Phillips)

Someone might observe that the disciples heard the challenge amid the pressure of that last week in Jerusalem and Jesus' pending death. Paul, on the other hand, had several years to digest and respond to the call to servanthood. Respond he did, and not just with words but with life. Paul associated Christian perfection with obedience and servanthood. At the close of his letter to the Philippians he addresses the need for obedience to God and servanthood. "Not that I claim to have achieved all this, nor to have reached perfection already. But I keep going on, trying to grasp that purpose for which Christ Jesus grasped me. My brothers, I do not consider myself to have grasped it fully even now. But I do concentrate on this: I forget all that lies behind me and with hands outstretched to whatever lies ahead I go straight for the goal—my reward, the honour of my high calling by God in Christ Jesus" (3:12-14). The "high calling" was the calling to be an obedient servant.

I worry about the world today because it is caught up in a power struggle. The church is affected as well. Regardless of whether it is with institutions or individuals, the sociologists agree that when power increases love decreases. The same is true when love

increases, power will decrease. Love and dominating power cannot
be expressed at the same time.

By observing his own family, a sociologist recently made some
interesting discoveries regarding the conflict between love and
controlling power. He points to his own extended family where a
number of divorces had occurred. His parents had divorced when he
was a teenager. He and his wife had divorced. Two of his children
had divorced their spouses. What happened? After careful analysis he
discovered that in each case the divorce was the result of "power"
and "love" games. The one who loved the least had the most
controlling power. You cannot express love and dominating power at
the same time.

Jesus knew this. If you are a follower of Jesus, it is not because you
were forced to do so by his power but because you were drawn to
Christ by his love. We love Jesus because he first loved us, because
he relinquished his power—"he emptied himself and became
obedient unto death." We are drawn to him. Jesus loved us more than
power. To be a Christian is to be an agent of love. You cannot be an
agent of God's love without relinquishing your power.

Jesus made this known the last night in the Upper Room. He took a
towel and a water basin and then proceeded to wash the feet of the
disciples. Those who think that Jesus is obsolete and irrelevant to life
today need to ponder this scene for a long time. Is there any issue
more important or more relevant to the beginning of the twenty-first
century than power?

The world seems to be sick to its heart with coercive power. It is
hungry to see strength demonstrated by service and love. Power that
exists for its own self-interest is being judged harshly. Perhaps the
world awaits a great nation that will come forth to lead the world not
by military might, but by compassionate service.

Wes Seeliger, in his parabolic book *Western Theology*, uses a
western vernacular to suggest that there are two kinds of Christians:
"Settler Christians" and "Pioneer Christians." The settler is more
institutional and bland. For example, the Settler church is described

as a courthouse where records are stored. The Pioneer church is a wagon train always on the move toward new frontiers.

Seeliger defines the Settler's concept of a pastor as a bank teller and the bishop was described as a bank president, sitting behind a big desk with a diamond stickpin in his tie. However, for the Pioneer church the pastor is defined and illustrated as the cook who feeds those on the wagon train. The bishop is the dishwasher, serving all the others. The Settler Christians were always being served. The Pioneer Christians were all servants.

Love is a greater force in history than power. Viktor Frankl proved this in the Nazi concentration camp where he was a prisoner during World War II. He writes that the Nazi guards would attempt to humiliate him by forcing him to wash the latrines with a tooth brush. Frankl shares that he would frustrate them by cleaning the latrines not once, but twice. When they asked him why he did that he told them, "The first time was because you made me do it. The second time was to show you that I love you." His actions finally dissipated the Nazi will to break him.

Christianity is the story of a servant people who, across twenty centuries, have been battered and beaten but refuse to die because, in fact, they are motivated by love and love cannot be destroyed by any power.

William Barclay describes a scene that took place on a train in Victoria Station in London, a few years after World War II. Barclay said that he was returning to Glasgow, when two young men boarded the train and were seated in the compartment he was occupying. Just after the train pulled out of the station, one of the men had an apparent epileptic seizure. He fell to the floor with a violent convulsion. He began to writhe and tremble. His young friend picked him up and put him back on the seat and wiped the beads of perspiration from his face. He placed a pillow behind his head and covered him with a blanket.

When his friend was somewhat calmed down, the attentive friend turned to Dr. Barclay and said, "I am sorry. I had hoped this would not happen. He has these seizures about twice a month, and he just had one a few days ago. We did not expect one so soon." Barclay responded by saying, "You need not apologize . . . I understand, no problem!"

"You can't really understand," the man responded. "My friend and I were in the Normandy invasion together. He is English, and I am an American. We were both wounded. My leg was blown off. My friend had shrapnel wounds all across his chest. A hand grenade had blown away much of his chest and shoulder." He continued his story, "I don't know how he did it, but he got to his feet and dragged me to safety. I heard him cry in agony each step of the way."

By this point the young American was very emotional. He said, "I kept telling him to go on and save himself, but he told me, 'no way. . . . If you die . . . I die with you,' and finally he got us to a medic station."

"Two years ago," he continued, "I found out that he had this condition. I am single. So I sold my house and furniture, quit my job, cashed in my savings, and came over here to take care of him because he needs around the clock attention. It's all right now, because I am with him, and I can serve him as long as he needs me."

William Barclay said, "Friend, you don't have to explain any more. That is the most beautiful and noble story that I have heard in my life." And the young man responded, "Man, you still don't understand. . . . After what he did for me . . . there isn't anything I would not do for him."

This is the call for all who follow Jesus. It is a call to take our lives and lay them on the line and say, "Whatever you want me to be, I will be! Wherever you want me to go, I will go! Whatever you want me to do, I will do! I am your faithful and obedient servant, as long as you need me."

5

Putting First Things First

His PRIORITIES Made Known

FIRST THINGS FIRST

*N*ow as they went on their way, he entered a certain village, where a woman named Martha welcomed him into her home. She had a sister named Mary, who sat at the Lord's feet and listened to what he was saying. But Martha was distracted by her many tasks; so she came to him and asked, "Lord, do you not care that my sister has left me to do all the work by myself? Tell her then to help me." But the Lord answered her, "Martha, Martha, you are worried and distracted by many things; there is need of only one thing. Mary has chosen the better part, which will not be taken away from her." (Luke 10:38-42 NRSV)

When all is said and done, what really matters to you?

Three days after Christmas in 1985, I suffered what the doctors diagnosed as a light heart attack. I was fifty-two years old. Six weeks later, I had triple by-pass surgery. Such an experience has a way of putting you in touch with your mortality in a hurry. Things that mattered a great deal don't mean much, and things too often taken for granted take on a greater dimension.

A friend introduced me to Robert Elliott's book *Is It Worth Dying For?* I purchased it and read it during my recovery period. The title was worth the price of the book. In the book, Elliott deals with coping with stress. He had suffered a heart attack at my same age. He believes that stress was the major contributing factor.

He does not dispute the fact that there are some things worth dying for, but often the things that cause the most stress and lead to our demise are not worth it. He states that we must determine what we are willing to die for. He said there are just two rules for life: "First, don't sweat the small stuff . . . and the second rule is that it is all small stuff.''

More than once Jesus took the opportunity to stress the importance of putting first things first.

''So don't worry and don't keep saying, 'What shall we eat, what shall we drink or what shall we wear?' That is what pagans are always looking for; your Heavenly Father knows that you need them all. Set your heart first on his kingdom and his goodness, and all these things will come to you as a matter of course'' (Matthew 6:31-33 Phillips).

When Jesus was in Bethany in the house of Simon the leper and sitting at the table, a woman approached him with an alabaster flask of very costly perfume. She poured the contents on Jesus' head. Some of the people present were distressed and asked, ''What is the point of such waste? The ointment could be sold and the money used to feed the poor.'' Jesus said, ''Let her alone, she has done a beautiful thing for me. Wherever the gospel is preached throughout the whole world, this act of hers will also be remembered'' (Matthew 26:13 paraphrase).

One of the most misquoted and misunderstood passages in Scripture is found in this same story. Jesus said, ''You have the poor with you always and you can do good to them whenever you like, but you will not always have me'' (vs. 11). Unfortunately, there are those who use this passage to justify the existence of the poor, as though God has decreed that they should always be. Jesus was simply saying, ''Get your priorities in order. In a few hours, I will no longer be with you. Use this time, as the woman used it, to express the devotion I need from you.''

On another occasion Jesus was visiting in Bethany and was invited to share a meal in the home of a woman named Martha. She had a sister named Mary who sat down at Jesus' feet, listening to what he had to say while Martha worked in the kitchen preparing the meal.

I recall from Sunday school days that Mary was lauded as the good example and Martha was the ''goat'' of the story. Through the years you have heard well-meaning people exalt the serious contemplative actions of Mary and downgrade Martha's attention to duty. This story was one of the factors that gave rise to the monastic life in the middle ages where attention to ''spiritual matters'' took precedence over the vulgarity of everyday life.

When the text is read carefully, one comes to understand that Martha is the central figure, not Mary. It is Martha's home, and she is the hostess. The meal takes place around her table. When you listen carefully to what Jesus is saying you discover that he is not praising Mary and condemning Martha. Jesus was attempting to explain Mary's need.

Jesus visiting in Martha's home was not by chance. She, more than likely, was a devoted follower. She took delight in preparing and serving food for Jesus and his companions. Mary's actions annoyed her and she said to Jesus, ''Lord, don't you mind that my sister has left me to do everything by myself? Tell her to come and help me!'' Jesus did not interpret Mary's behavior as lazy or selfish. He saw her as a seeker of the truth. He saw Martha, unlike Mary, as a more mature disciple. He seemed to be saying, ''Martha, my dear, you are worried and bothered about Mary not helping with the meal. The preparation of the meal is important, but Mary doesn't need to be in the kitchen tonight. Be patient. There is not anything more important than what she is doing right now.'' Jesus supported Mary in her choice to listen at his feet, but at the same time, he demonstrated the highest regard for Martha.

Jesus took the opportunity at the meal table to make known the importance of putting first things first. These priorities will not be the same for every person at a given moment. At times prayer and contemplation should take precedence in our lives, but at other times we need to get up off our knees and go into the world to tend to those who need our help.

This was true with John Wesley's break with the Fetter Lane Society in London. They had become a pious group who did not see the need for doing anything other than praying and singing. Because of this, he severed his relation with them and embarked on his field preaching enterprise.

There has always been the tension between these two expressions of faith: good works and faith. Jesus was affirming both in Martha's home in Bethany. There is a time for getting your priorities in order in relation to what is most needed in our lives at the moment.

In each of the Synoptic Gospels, Jesus is reported spending most of his ministry in the Galilee area. Then he reaches a point where "he sets his face toward Jerusalem" (see Matthew 20:17; Mark 10:32; Luke 9:51). John has Jesus and his disciples going in and out of Jerusalem on several occasions. The Synoptics record only one journey to Jerusalem, just before his Crucifixion.

Just prior to his account of the story of the meal in Martha's home in Bethany (Luke 10:38-42), Luke intentionally relates several events that lead up to the account with Martha and Mary. Jesus' decision to go to Jerusalem was a priority choice. He had to decide between Galilee and Jerusalem, and he made his choice. Three events during his journey make known priority choices that must be made by Jesus' followers. They are important because they all address Jesus' insistence on putting first things first.

The first event took place as Jesus and his disciples made their way through the Samaritan villages. As the little company made its way along the road, a man came up to Jesus and said, "I'm going to follow you wherever you go." Jesus' response was, "Follow me."

The man replied, "Let me go and bury my father first." But Jesus told him, "Leave the dead to bury the dead. You must first come away and preach the kingdom of God."

Another man approached him, "I'm going to follow you, Lord, but first let me bid farewell to my people at home."

Jesus told him, "Anyone who puts his hand to the plough and then looks behind him is useless for the kingdom of God" (Luke 9:59-62).

Jesus was saying, "If you are going to follow me you must commit your life to me unreservedly."

St. Columba and his disciples understood this kind of commitment. They landed on the isle of Iona off the coast of Scotland in the sixth century. This marked the first time that Christian missionaries successfully established themselves in the British Isles. There had been other attempts, but the feared Norsemen either killed them or forced them to retreat. When St. Columba and his disciples landed they destroyed their boats. They wanted no means of escape. Their commitment to their mission to preach the gospel among the inhabitants of the Isles was first and foremost and nothing was to prevent it.

One can find throughout the Synoptics the passages of Jesus using the expression, "Follow me." He uttered these words to Peter and Andrew as he met them by the side of the Galilean Sea. To them he said, "Come, follow me, and I will make you fishers of men." They left their nets and followed him. He found Matthew at the seat of the Customs, and he said, "Come follow me." And we know that Matthew followed.

To all who would follow him he challenged, "Deny yourselves, take up your cross and follow me." This has been true throughout the nearly two thousand years of the Christian mission. Jesus' call, to "follow me," is a call to commit our lives unreservedly to him. The residents of the Samaritan villages were not the only audience. Jesus was hoping that the disciples who had earlier answered the call to follow him would hear what he was saying loud and clear. As they made their way toward Jerusalem, Jesus must have sensed their ambiguity. They were looking for a way out of their commitment.

When Jesus said, "Come, follow me," he was issuing an invitation, not a demand. That invitation excited those who first heard it. It sounded like someone who was going somewhere and knew where he was going. The invitation was, "come follow me, and you can be a part of this." He was more interested in their present and future than he was in their past.

Most importantly, he does not call us to go somewhere alone; he says "follow me . . . I'll show you the way . . . I'll go with you all the way . . . even to the end of the earth . . ."

Leadership like that is inspiring. It was a leadership that came through authority, not coercive power. An authority earned by sacrificial service is the kind of leadership that Jesus expects all of us to give when we follow him. It is servant leadership.

Kenneth Goodson, a United Methodist bishop in Alabama during the civil rights struggles of the sixties, was such a leader. His leadership was so inspiring and courageous that it was said of him, "We will charge the gates of hell with a water pistol if he asks."

Booker T. Washington was another such leader. As the President of Tuskegee Institute in Alabama, he was dedicated to teaching young African-Americans to be self sustaining in their life following the Civil War.

Linda McMurry in *George Washington Carver: Scientist and Symbol,* relates how it was the concern of Dr. Washington to find someone who would come and help these people to learn agriculture. He knew how to teach them to build buildings and to read and write, but he needed someone to come and show them how to grow corn. He needed someone like George Washington Carver.

George Washington Carver was born a slave. He struggled to attain his education and later became a distinguished member of the faculty at Iowa State University.

When Booker T. Washington was on a fund raising trip through the Midwest, according to McMurry, he visited Iowa, and asked to see Dr. Carver. As these two famous men were introduced to each other, Washington said, "You are the man who can come and do for my school and my people what needs to be done. I cannot offer you much in the way of a salary. But I can offer you the greatest challenge in the world."

Dr. Washington went back to Tuskegee and wrote Carver a letter, and once again spelled out his challenge. "As I told you before I cannot offer you much. But how I need you. How God needs you to be here in this particular place and at this time to help these people."

George Washington Carver took the letter and walked out on the campus to a little garden grove. There he sat down in a secluded place and read the letter again. Then he took a little writing tablet and wrote three words, signed it, and sent it to Dr. Washington at Tuskegee Institute, Tuskegee, Alabama. Washington read the letter. "I will come" were the only words. The letter was signed, "Your servant, George Washington Carver."

Jesus invites us to do no less. "Come follow me. . . ."

The second event among the Samaritan villages, wherein Jesus stresses the importance of placing first things first, takes place when he dispatches seventy persons to go out and preach and heal the sick. " 'There is a great harvest,' he told them, 'but only a few are working in it—which means you must pray to the Lord of the harvest that he will send out more reapers to bring in his harvest' " (Luke 10:2).

Jesus was clearly saying if you are going to be my follower you must witness to your faith unashamedly.

Jesus gave a mini-workshop on witnessing. He did not speak of programs or techniques of evangelism. He did not mention any skills that a Christian witness must acquire. He simply said, "Go on your way and live the faith among the people, sharing with them the good news that the kingdom is near."

It is obvious from these verses that it is of utmost importance for all followers to share their faith, to witness unashamedly. Jesus addressed the fact that too few were witnessing. He said that the workers were (and are) few.

Recently, while I was visiting in Denmark, I accompanied a group of university students to one of the busy squares in the heart of Copenhagen for the purpose of participating in some street evangelism. I was apprehensive when I was invited, because I did not know what their methods might be. Some so-called evangelistic tactics make me uncomfortable.

There were about twenty of us in the team. There were instrumentalists, singers, storytellers, and dancers. They sang contemporary songs, performed pantomime and interpretive dance. People who passed by stopped for a while and engaged the young people in conversation. There was never any high powered or

61

aggressive pursuit of anyone. They shared their faith with persons who inquired. They invited persons to Christ and their church. When it was appropriate, they shared Christian literature with passers-by. They do this each Saturday afternoon. Hundreds of young adults are making commitments to Christ and returning to the church. This was one of the most effective ventures in street evangelism that I have witnessed. Nothing fancy. Just young Christians being honest, caring, and unashamedly witnessing to their faith in Christ in an unlikely place.

Jesus had some pretty hard words for the people of Bethsaida, Chorazin, and Capernaum. His harsh words were due to the fact that he had spent more time in these three cities than anywhere else. He said, "For if Tyre and Sidon had seen the demonstrations of God's power that you have seen, they would have repented long ago." (vs. 13). They were hearers of the Word, but they were not willing to witness to the Word.

One cannot help seeing a parallel to the institutional church in the Western world. It is impossible to fathom the resources, both human and financial, showered on the institutional church in North America and Europe. It is mind boggling to imagine what would happen if those resources could be applied to the growing church in Asia or Africa.

This is the same issue that Jesus was addressing in the passage recorded in Luke 10:1-16. We have not placed witnessing to our faith as a priority. Jesus makes it crystal clear that we are to put first things first by witnessing to our faith in Christ unashamedly.

Erasmus, the Renaissance scholar, is given credit for a mythical tale, told to emphasize the importance of carrying out the evangelistic mandate. In the story, Jesus returns to heaven after his time on earth. The angels gather around him to learn of the events that occurred during his days on earth. Jesus tells them of his miracles, his teachings, and his death and Resurrection. When he finishes his story, Michael, the Archangel, asks, "But what happens now?"

Jesus answers, "I have left behind eleven faithful disciples and a handful of men and women who have faithfully followed me. They will declare my message and express my love. These faithful people will build my church."

"But," responds Michael, "what if these people fail? What then is your other plan?"

Jesus' answer was to the point, "I have no other plan."

For better or worse, we who are now members of the body of Christ are the instruments God has chosen to spread his word and build his kingdom.

The third event that Luke includes in the tenth chapter and just prior to the story of the meal in Martha's home in Bethany is the parable that we have come to know as the good Samaritan.

One of the experts in the Law stood up to test Jesus and said, "Master, what must I do to be sure of eternal life?" Jesus asked what the Law requires. The man responded by saying, "The Law says, 'Thou shalt love the Lord thy God with all thy heart and with all thy soul and with all thy strength and with all thy mind . . . and thy neighbor as thyself.' "

"Quite right," said Jesus. "Do that and you will live."

But the man, wanting to justify himself, continued, "But who is my 'neighbor'?"

Jesus told the familiar story known as the parable of the good Samaritan. After describing the Samaritan as the unexpected doer of good deeds, Jesus said to the man, "Now go and do the same for others."

Jesus makes it known that he expects his disciples to put a high priority on loving people unconditionally. This was his own example. Jesus never derided or disdained any person. Every act on his part was one of unconditional love. The parable of the good Samaritan was a wonderful example of Jesus' value for persons.

When Luke follows these events with the scene at the supper table in Martha's home in Bethany, his readers understood unequivocally what aspect of Jesus' teaching Luke was underscoring. We must put first things first. The three events leading up to the scene in Martha's home underscore three high priorities for Jesus:

1. We are to *commit our lives unreservedly* (the story of not looking back—not burying parents and so on).
2. We are to *witness to our faith unashamedly* (the story of witnessing).
3. We are to *love people unconditionally* (the story of the good Samaritan).

Søren Kierkegaard, the Danish theologian, tells a story that happened in a jewelry store in Copenhagen. A thief broke into the store one evening. He did not take anything from the store. He simply switched the price tags and waited around until the next morning to observe the confusion. Expensive pieces of jewelry had very low price tags and simple costume jewelry had high price tags.

Kierkegaard theorizes on what would happen if we could switch price tags in the church. Ministries that are given a greater value may not be that valuable in the light of the gospel, and ministries that receive little value may deserve the greatest.

Jesus' priorities for discipleship were clearly made known. Disciples are to commit their lives to following Christ unreservedly, to witnessing for Christ unashamedly, and to loving people unconditionally. When we do these we will be putting first things first.

6

Plenty Good Room at My Father's Table

JUSTICE Made Known

"DOING JUSTICE...CLEANS THE INSIDE"

*W*hile he was speaking, a Pharisee invited him to dine with him; so he went in and took his place at the table. The Pharisee was amazed to see that he did not first wash before dinner. Then the Lord said to him, "Now you Pharisees clean the outside of the cup and of the dish, but inside you are full of greed and wickedness. You fools! Did not the one who made the outside make the inside also? So give for alms those things that are within; and see, everything will be clean for you.

"But woe to you Pharisees! For you tithe mint and rue and herbs of all kinds, and neglect justice and the love of God; it is these you ought to have practiced, without neglecting the others. Woe to you Pharisees! For you love to have the seat of honor in the synagogues and to be greeted with respect in the marketplaces. Woe to you! For you are like unmarked graves, and people walk over them without realizing it." (Luke 11:37-44 NRSV)

The date was September 18, 1990, the twenty-ninth anniversary of the tragic death of Dag Hammarskjöld. My wife and I stood beside his grave in Uppsala, Sweden. He is one of the heroes of the twentieth century, a man who stood for justice in the world. He was on a mission of justice when his plane crashed near Ndola, Northern Rhodesia. He was negotiating a cease fire between UN forces and the forces of the Katanga province of what was known then as the Republic of the Congo.

The inscription on his gravemarker are his own words. "Justice must be done. Every human being deserves justice. Some people are powerless to attain what is equitable and fair in life. It behooves the person of faith and conscience to stand with those who are treated unjustly."

I remember singing around the campfire an old spiritual "Plenty

Good Room.'' The words mean more to me now than they did when I was a teenager. "Plenty good room in ma Father's Kingdom, . . . just choose your seat and sit down.'' The African-American slaves sang this spiritual when they were denied a place in society. They longed for the time when they would have a "place at the table.''

Once when Jesus was the dinner guest in the home of a Pharisee, he made known, in dramatic terms, his concern for love and justice.

Late in the afternoon, while Jesus was speaking on the theme of sincerity, he was interrupted by a heckler. The rude heckler was the Pharisee who later that evening became Jesus' dinner host. Jesus was accustomed to interruptions, but this marked the first time a heckler invited him to supper.

Luke records that soon after Jesus arrived, the conversation became heated. No mention is given that they ever got around to eating. It may be that when Jesus finished with them, they lost their appetites. When they gathered around the table, the Pharisee challenged Jesus as to why he did not wash before the meal. It was not Jesus' social graces or his hygiene that concerned the host. It was Jesus' apparent disregard for the purification laws of Israel. The law required that people wash their hands seven times in preparation for a meal. The Pharisee may have been upset that Jesus only washed once. This criticism was but one more addressed to Jesus and his disciples.

This verbal attack was a mistake, because Jesus responded with one of his most scorching rebukes leveled at the Pharisees and their scribes. He started out by saying, "You Pharisees are fond of cleaning the outside of your cups and dishes, but inside yourselves you are full of greed and wickedness! Have you no sense? Don't you realise that the one who made the outside is the maker of the inside as well?''

In other words, the Pharisees tried to give the right appearances, but they were corrupt deep down in their heart of hearts.

Jesus continued, "If you would only make the inside clean by giving the contents to those in need, the outside becomes clean as a matter of course.'' Jesus does not let up, "But alas for you Pharisees, for you pay out your tithe of mint and rue and every little herb, and lose sight of the justice and the love of God '' (Luke 11:40-42).

It is of little surprise that when Jesus left the house, the scribes and Pharisees began to nurture a bitter hatred against him. He left them with a bad case of contempt . . . and probably indigestion.

Jesus' key words for the Pharisees, "If you would only make the inside clean by *giving the contents to those in need, . . .*" are a call to do justice. Do not make the mistake of interpreting this to mean only a call to deeper piety or a spiritual cleansing, as important as this may be. Jesus stressed that the two should not be separated. It is a call to *do justice*. He had problems with those who lifted themselves as the religious pure but had little compassion for doing justice in the world.

Later in Luke's account of the gospel, Jesus warns his disciples against religious pretentiousness: "Be on your guard against the scribes, who enjoy walking around in long robes and love having men bow to them in public, getting front seats in the synagogue, and the best places at dinner parties—while all the while they are devouring widows' property and covering it up with lengthy prayers. These men are only heading for deeper damnation" (Luke 20:46-47 NRSV). In the twenty-third chapter of Matthew, we read, "Alas for you, scribes and Pharisees, you utter frauds! For you pay your tithe on mint and dill and cumin, and neglect the things which carry far more weight in the Law—justice, mercy and good faith. These are the things you should have observed—without neglecting others. You are blind leaders, for you filter out a mosquito yet swallow a camel" (Matthew 23:23-24).

Jesus seemed to be saying to the Pharisees and scribes, "You cannot divorce faith from life; religious observance from acts of love and justice; and for Christian disciples, the gospel from the world."

There is some danger in reading about the behavior of the Pharisees. We run the risk of enjoying attacking their sins and never relating their behavior to our condition in the church. There are some contemporary Christians who identify first-century Pharisaism with present day Judaism, which is an error. It may be that a more accurate comparison can be drawn between first-century Pharisaism and certain expressions and practices of the institutional church today.

Pharisees were Jewish laymen who took their religion seriously.

They had some pretty high standards. They believed religion should relate to the whole of life, not just to Temple sacrifices or sabbath observances or occasional celebrations. Being serious, dedicated men, they wanted the Laws of God to be applied to the whole range of human life. Their peak of prominence and power was reached one hundred years before Christ. Because their great desire was to live before God as good, righteous, and holy men, they felt it necessary to separate themselves more and more from all that would defile. Their name itself means "the separated ones." Their love of the synagogue and its worship was well-known, and keeping God's laws was their passion.

The apostle Paul was once an ardent member of their company. Several of Jesus' disciples were Pharisees. The "Bethsaida Five," Peter, Andrew, James, John, and Philip, were all Pharisees. Traditionally, Bethsaida was a very conservative religious community, well versed in keeping the Law. Knowing this is to realize that one of Jesus' primary concerns was that his own disciples would understand the importance of doing justice. He was as eager for them to hear as he was for the Pharisees who accompanied him wherever he went.

The basic concern is the definition of authentic religion. The Pharisees believed that obedience to law was supreme. Jesus challenged this idea stating that such legalism reduces religion to a set of rules. That is why he claimed that the Pharisees should be concerned with cleansing their hearts as well as washing their hands. To do so would make them better people and more sensitive to the needs of others. Jesus' concern was not so much the religious practice of the Pharisees as it was that they had a religion they *could* practice.

The Pharisees developed an elaborate scheme around each law to ensure that there were enough exceptions built into the law that they would not transgress. When religion gets this strung out on details and technicalities, then we have forgotten what true religion is all about—namely, our relationship with God.

Jesus focused on the great moral obligations of life, such as love of God and justice among persons. This is more difficult and leaves us humble, because we never can live up to these demands. These moral obligations are not scored like the Pharisee's boasting to God . . . "I thank you that I am not like others. . . . I fast . . . I pray . . . I give tithes . . ." (Luke 18:12 paraphrase). Jesus' words and deeds emphasized love and justice as the primary agenda for his followers.

Unlike the Pharisees and their scribes, Jesus used the meal table to demonstrate and to make known that issues of justice should be greater concerns than rituals and tradition. When the Pharisees asked him why he ate with sinners and other outcasts, Jesus said the "healthy" do not need a doctor, but those who are ill do. At the beginning of Jesus' ministry, he identified himself with the poor, the blind, the captives, the bruised (Luke 4:18); and he spoke out for widows on different occasions.

New insight has come from biblical archaeology that provides understanding of the biblical record of the struggle for justice. There are over 240 major tells in Israel today. Each tell contains the remains of an ancient city. Most explorations of these tells have occurred since 1948, the time of independence for the modern state of Israel. Fewer than fifty major archaeological digs have been attempted.

They have made an interesting discovery. The masses of people did not live within the city walls. They lived on the outside. Only the royalty and wealthier citizens lived inside.

In the Old Testament, there are numerous references to "daughters of Judah" or "daughters of Jerusalem" or "daughters of Israel." This does not mean the female offspring. The people of the land or the poor were known as the "daughters" of the cities. These people did not have the protection of the city wall when the enemy came. They often were shut out and powerless.

When the enemy approached the city, the warning was sounded, and the people gathered within the city walls. The gates were closed, and the people prepared for the enemy besiegement. Many of the peasants who lived outside of the walls were denied protection within the walls. They were left to be destroyed by the approaching enemy armies. It was the duty of the prophet to stand at the city gate and plead for the rights of the "daughters." The "haves" were secure within the walls and the "have nots" were shut out.

It has always been the tradition of the prophets of God to advocate for the "daughters" of the world, for those who are powerless to stand for themselves, for the outcasts and forgotten people, the powerless. In Jackson, Mississippi, for example, Episcopalians, Roman Catholics, and United Methodists have joined in establishing a nursing home for people with AIDS. No nursing home in the state of Mississippi will admit people with AIDS. People have been generous in helping these "daughters" who have very little advocacy. Oftentimes there are no acceptable places for people with AIDS to die.

Jesus declared with his words and actions that people of faith were to stand by the powerless. He was grieved that the Pharisees and their scribes ignored this obligation. Jesus was disappointed in the Pharisees and scribes, who came from the tradition of the prophets, for not caring for their "daughters." Jesus scolded them, "You follow all of the rules, but you lose sight of justice. You should keep God's Law, but issues of love and justice ought to be your concern as well."

A powerful story comes out of Warsaw just prior to Hitler's invasion. A Quaker missionary nurse was stationed in the ghetto of that city. Loved by all, she served in a Roman Catholic community even though she was a Quaker. When she became ill and died, the whole community grieved.

Where she was to be buried became a problem. There were no Protestant cemeteries—only a Roman Catholic and a Jewish cemetery. Strict burial laws stated that only Catholics could be buried in the Catholic cemetery, only Jews in the Jewish cemetery. Religious leaders of both denied burial of the woman. Finally, the Roman Catholic bishop agreed for her body to be buried just outside the cemetery fence.

The people agreed to the conditions. After a beautiful resurrection service attended by thousands, they carried her body to the Roman Catholic cemetery and buried it just outside the fence.

An interesting thing happened during the night. Some of the people in the ghetto went out under the cover of darkness and moved the fence so that her grave was inside the fence.

Jesus made it known that this was his ministry and his expectation of all who were to be his disciples: We are called to "move the fence" so that the "daughters" of the world will be included.

People of faith have always inquired of what God expects from them. In the sixth chapter of Micah the people ask, "Does God wish burnt offerings, calves a year old? What about a thousand rams, with ten thousand rivers of oil? Shall I give my first born for my transgressions? What does the Lord require of me . . . ?" Micah's answer was succinct: "The Lord requires of you to do justice, to love mercy, and to walk humbly with God" (Micah 6:6-8 paraphrase). These words of the Old Testament prophet come close to the message of Jesus.

Jesus was more than a prophet but his message was in the tradition of the prophets of justice. The problem with Pharisees past and present is they believe that keeping rules and traditions is more important than the "daughters" having access to the city or, what is more important, to the table.

In his book *A Reasonable Faith*, Anthony Campolo shares an incident that happened when he was teaching sociology at the University of Pennsylvania. He was teaching a course entitled Social Problems, and in that course, he reviewed a variety of the pathologies of society ranging from alcoholism to child abuse.

One day, in order to get class discussion going, he asked his students what some of the world's great religious leaders might have said about prostitution. He asked what Buddha or Muhammad might have said on the subject. He asked what the Mosaic Law had to say about this dehumanizing practice. The discussion was lively and intense. Then he asked what Jesus would have said to a prostitute.

A Jewish student answered, "Jesus never met a prostitute."

Dr. Campolo picked up his New Testament and responded, "Yes he did. I'll show you in the Bible."

The young man interrupted him again. "You didn't hear me, Doctor. I said Jesus never met a prostitute."

Once again Campolo protested. Once again he reached for his New Testament and started to leaf through the pages searching for passages that showed Jesus forgiving the "fallen woman." He turned to the passage where he gave the woman at the well a chance for spiritual renewal.

Once again, the student spoke out, this time with a touch of anger in his raised voice. "You are not listening to me, sir. You are not listening to what I am saying. I am saying that Jesus never met a prostitute. Do you think that when he looked at Mary Magdalene she was a prostitute? Do you think he saw whores when he looked at women like her? Doctor, listen to me! Jesus never met a prostitute."

The teacher fell silent. The teacher was being corrected by a student who understood Christ's message more than some seasoned Christians.

To be a Christian is to learn to see people as Christ sees them. When the church is really the body of Christ, its members accept things that the world cannot accept. The "daughters" are of primary concern. The prostitute becomes a sister. The convicted criminal becomes a brother. The outsider becomes an insider.

Giacomo Puccini, the renowned Italian operatic composer, died in 1924. He was in the midst of composing *Turandot*. He died with the composition only half complete. His students, primarily Franco Alfano and Arturo Toscanini, completed the opera.

Toscanini directed the first performance of *Turandot* in the Milan Opera House in 1926. Half way through the performance, Toscanini turned to the audience and said, "To this point you have witnessed the work of our master teacher, Giacomo Puccini. Now, you shall witness the work of his devoted students and disciples." He turned and directed the magnificent conclusion to *Turandot*, written and conducted by the faithful followers of Puccini.

Our Master has shown us the way. The work for justice is incomplete. It is not enough for the Christian to decry injustice, we must work to eliminate it. It is not enough to deplore poverty and need, we must help to create a society where poverty and hunger no longer exist. It is not enough to lament racism in our society, we must become change agents in our communities to eradicate racism in all its subtle forms. It is not enough to wish for peace, we must work for peace by becoming peacemakers.

7

How Much Is "So Much"?

LOVE Made Known

"GOD LOVED THE WORLD SO MUCH"

*O*ne night Nicodemus, a leading Jew and Pharisee, came to see Jesus. "Rabbi," he began, "we realise that you are a teacher who has come from God. For no one could show the signs that you show unless God were with him."

"Believe me," returned Jesus, "when I assure you that a man cannot see the kingdom of God without being born again."

"And how can a man who has grown old possibly be born?" replied Nicodemus. "Surely he cannot go into his mother's womb a second time to be born?"

"I do assure you," said Jesus, "that unless a man is born from water and from spirit he cannot enter the kingdom of God. Flesh gives birth to flesh and spirit gives birth to spirit: you must not be surprised that I told you that all of you must be born again. The wind blows where it likes, you can hear the sound of it, but you have no idea where it comes from or where it goes. Nor can you tell how a man is born by the wind of the Spirit."

"How on earth can things like this happen?" replied Nicodemus.

"So you are the teacher of Israel," said Jesus, "and you do not understand such things? I assure you that we are talking about what we know and we are witnessing to what we have observed, yet you will not accept our evidence. Yet if I have spoken to you about things which happen on this earth and you will not believe me, what chance is there that you will believe me if I tell you about what happens in Heaven? No one has ever been up to Heaven except the Son of Man who came down from Heaven. The Son of Man must be lifted above the heads of men—as Moses lifted up that serpent in the desert—so that any man who believes in him may have eternal life. For God loved the world so much that he gave his only Son, so that everyone who believes in him should not be lost, but should have eternal life. God has not sent his Son into the world to pass sentence upon it, but to save it—through him. (John 3:1-17 Phillips)

A hell-fire-and-brimstone preacher was giving one of his typical sermons and was laying it on the people. Using some of the apocalyptic texts from the Gospel according to Matthew, he said, "And in the day of judgment, you sinners will be cast into outer darkness, and there will be weeping, and there will be wailing, and you will gnash your teeth."

When he paused to get his breath, an elderly woman in the third row raised a timid hand and said, "But preacher, some of us don't have teeth." To which he replied, "Don't worry, lady, on judgment day teeth will be provided."

Loose interpretation of Scripture like that is probably what gets us into trouble and creates more conflicts among Christians than any other thing.

The history of biblical interpretation is a fascinating discipline and an important one. Frequently, scholars use two words I shall now use simply because all of us should know and understand them. The words are *exegesis* and *eisegesis*. They are Greek words. *Exegesis* means to draw out the meaning of Scripture, to guide through finding its basic, true, or original meaning. *Eisegesis* means to read ideas and interpretations into Scripture—ideas not there. It has come to mean imposing our own ideas upon Scripture. Any Bible interpreter concerned with integrity keeps this distinction in mind and works hard to be honest in exegesis and, at the least, acknowledges what is being done when indulging in eisegesis.

The third chapter of John is worthy of sound exegesis. The sixteenth verse, "For God loved the world so much that he gave his only Son, so that everyone who believes in him should not be lost, but should have eternal life" (John 3:16 Phillips) is among the most beloved and most quoted verses in all Scripture. A verse such as this, stored in the memories of millions throughout the years, must contain some basic truth that needs to be studied and understood by all of us.

Good exegesis demands that we understand more than the words that are written. When readers understand the environment and circumstances surrounding a passage, they are better prepared to understand the deeper meaning.

In this passage, there are some things that point to the setting and circumstances surrounding the immanent meeting of the learned Nicodemus, a leading Pharisee, with Jesus.

Nicodemus came to Jesus in secret. It was nighttime. He was a man of considerable position and influence among the Pharisees. He was a member of the Sanhedrin, the ruling body of elders in Jerusalem. Apparently he did not wish his colleagues to know of his visit to this teacher, whose message and miracles were arousing the people to the extent that the Pharisees were taking steps to stop him. Nicodemus wanted to get from Jesus a further sign that he was a unique teacher. He had seen evidence in the miracles that Jesus was no fly-by-night rabbi. He had heard enough of his teaching to inquire further. So now he comes to Jesus in the concealing darkness.

Jesus was the host. Even though Jesus did not own a home in or near Jerusalem, he had access to one, just as he did in Capernaum. Nicodemus sought him out and visited him late at night. Jesus, the host, would provide refreshments, according to custom. Probably bread, fruit, and wine. The late Dr. Albert Barnett, professor of New Testament at Emory University, said this was the only "midnight snack" mentioned in the Scriptures. The setting was on the roof-top where Jesus and Nicodemus, alone, were able to enjoy the cool evening breezes that blew in from the Mediterranean. Overhead were the moon and stars against the black background of the sky.

For Christians, the account of Jesus and Nicodemus usually brings to mind the wonderful dialogue about spiritual rebirth. When Nicodemus acknowledged the greatness of Jesus' teaching and his amazement over the signs and wonders of his ministry, Jesus stunned him with his response. He told the learned Pharisee that if the new life that God can bring into the human heart is to be lived, there must be a new creature, wholly new . . . as if born anew. In fact, he states it simply in the Scripture, "Believe me," Jesus said, "when I assure you that a man cannot see the kingdom of God without being born again" (John 3:3). Jesus was saying that one must, in one's spiritual life, experience a new birth. Jesus was telling Nicodemus about God's free gift of salvation. Here is the grace of God that offers to anyone in any age the gift of life eternal. This is the redeeming grace that alone can assure anyone of membership in God's kingdom. The gift is available for all who, by means of spiritual rebirth, enter into the kingdom.

Nicodemus was full of questions. "How on earth can things like this happen?" he asked. Jesus did his best to answer his questions. Jesus used the gentle breezes to explain the movement of God's spirit. One of the most important answers he gave is often taken out of context. When quoting John 3:16, very few people relate the text to Jesus' conversation with Nicodemus. It is usually quoted as though it is not related to anything else. Some call the verse "the gospel in miniature."

When Nicodemus asked Jesus, "How on earth can a person experience spiritual renewal?" Jesus answered with the words, "For God loved the world so much that he gave his only Son, so that everyone who believes in him should not be lost, but should have eternal life. God has not sent his Son into the world to pass sentence on it, but to save it—through him" (John 3:16-17 Phillips).

The words that leap out at me in the text are the words *so much*. It could have read, "God loved the world." That would have been enough, but an intensity is added by the words, *so much*. A deeper significance comes when one exegetically examines the kind of love that the words *so much* describe.

The Hebrews and the Greeks pave the way for Christian thought. The word *love* is a fusion of Hebrew and Hellenistic thought. The Jews contributed the concept of God, the supreme being. The Greeks contributed the concept of love. But it was Christianity that first made the connection between God and love.

We seem to take the revelation of God and love for granted. We have seen "God is love" on everything from bumper stickers to painted overpasses on interstate highways. It is a foundational Christian doctrine. What a wonderful thing that has come from this teaching. Over a billion Orthodox, Catholic, and Protestant Christians still adhere to the teaching that God is love.

When Jesus shared with Nicodemus that "God loved the world *so much* that he gave his only Son . . .," he was describing a special kind of love that Nicodemus had not heard about.

The first awakenings to the idea that God and love are integral centered around the Greek word *nomos*. *Nomos* means law. The concept of love in *nomos* is reciprocal. In other words, a person submits to God's will and shows obedience through actions. God, in turn, will bless the person. This reciprocal relationship with God was the Hebrew idea of divine-human love.

Nicodemus was familiar with the many Old Testament stories that demonstrated that kind of love. There are many examples where love for God is demonstrated through acts of submission, obedience, and sacrifice; and God in turn blesses that faithfulness by providing for and dealing justly with the faithful. It is a love through adherence to law. Being a strict Pharisee, Nicodemus understood this concept, but he knew that this was not the love of God that Jesus was talking about.

Another kind of love that can be found in the Old Testament was a divine-human love idea that was more powerful than *nomos*. It was called *philia*. Love to Aristotle and Plato was a fellowship of like-minded persons. *Philia* is a loving, harmonious relationship. Aristotle was always looking for what he called the ideal or true friend.

The Christian church is such a group of such persons. Paul spoke of being in Christ among the community of believers. The church is a fellowship of love. *Philia* is evident throughout the New Testament.

There are examples in the Old Testament as well. Near the end of II Samuel there is a brief vignette from the life of David that describes an act of love that is a perfect description of *philia*. Nicodemus would have been familiar with this story.

David is an old man and is forced to go to war once more against his old foes the Philistines. He gathers his soldiers together at Adullam, and the enemy encamps at Bethlehem, which had been David's childhood home. That evening, as David looks out across the enemy lines at his childhood city far off in the distance, he says to himself with a sigh, "Oh, if only I could drink once more from the waters of Bethlehem. . . ."

There are three soldiers standing near who overhear their beloved king, and they decide to answer his wish. They crawl out of the camp, cross behind enemy lines and bring back a pitcher of water from the well at Bethlehem.

They are attacked and wounded in the process but manage to escape. Bloodied and exhausted, they bring the king the water for which he had asked.

But David does not drink it. Instead he says . . . "How can I drink water that has cost such a price?" And he pours the water out on the ground as an offering to God. It was sacred in his sight, and so, in gratitude to God, he made it into an offering. David was overwhelmed with astonishment to find out that someone loved him that much, that someone would do such a dangerous thing for him without being ordered to do it. They did it because they loved him and knew it would give him pleasure.

There is a manifestation of love in this brief biblical story that the whole world needs. A love that causes you to do something that you do not have to do. A love that enables you to care for someone or give yourself to someone, not because you have to or because you are expected to, but because you want to . . . for the sake of love.

Nicodemus knew about such love. Perhaps he had been the recipient of such love. Maybe he had extended that kind of love to others. He may have believed that his secret visit with Jesus was to impart brotherly concern and love. He knew that the love that Jesus was speaking of was much greater than anything he had heard of in the synagogues or seen demonstrated by the most Godly people he knew.

The Christian community had to come up with a completely different word to define what Jesus meant when he told Nicodemus that "God loved the world so much. . . ." The word is *agape*. It, too, is a Greek word. The word did not exist before New Testament times.

Agape takes us out of the exclusiveness of *philia* love and removes it from the submissiveness of *nomos*. *Agape* love is that love which is demonstrated so majestically in Christ, but *agape* love can only come through a human being. It cannot come through laws nor even the institution of the church. If you don't get it through the one next to you or someone else who has received the love of God through Christ, then you may not get it.

The story is told that when the Roman Empire was at its height there was a mutinous young general named Cagular who lived on the island we know as Sicily. He refused to give complete allegiance to the emperor. His legions were loyal to their general. After a number of attempts to persuade Cagular to be an obedient servant to the emperor, several Roman legions were dispatched to bring this renegade general to justice. He was captured and, along with his family, placed in chains and transported to Rome to be tried.

Cagular feared the worst for himself and his family. When he finally stood with his family before the emperor, a strange turn of events took place. The emperor was so affected with Cagular's handsome family that he offered a gesture of leniency.

The emperor asked Cagular what he would do if he spared his life. Cagular responded by saying, "Sir, if you should spare my life, I would return to my place of duty and serve you obediently, for the rest of my days."

"What would you do if I should spare the life of your children?"

"Sir, if you should spare the life of my precious children, I would rally my legions and lead them into battle wherever you command."

The emperor was impressed with the answers. Then he asked a final question. "What would you do if I should spare the life of your wife?"

Then Cagular, with tears, said, "Sir, if you should spare the life of my dear wife, I will be willing to die for you."

The emperor was so moved by Cagular's responses that he pardoned him and sent him back to his duties. As the family made their return trip, Cagular and his wife spoke of their visit to Rome and the palace.

Cagular asked his wife, "Did you see the beautiful tapestries in the emperor's court?"

His wife responded, "No, I did not see them."

"What about the solid gold statues lining the corridors. Do you remember seeing them?"

"No, I didn't see them," she answered.

"Surely you saw the elegant woodwork in the throne room!"

Again, she simply answered, "No, I did not see that."

Then Cagular, annoyed with her answers, said, "Woman, if you did not see the magnificent works of beauty, what did you see?"

Her answer was simple. "I saw only the face of the man who said he loved me enough to die for me."

Magnify this a trillion times and you begin to get a glimpse of what Jesus was saying to Nicodemus that night long ago.

When we look into the face of Christ on the cross, we see *agape* in action. Nicodemus, and the world, were not ready for such a love. Nicodemus asked, "How on earth can people be changed into new creatures?" Jesus said, "It is possible because God loved the world so much that he gave his only Son, so that everyone who believes in him should not be lost, but should have eternal life." This is what Isaac Watts knew first hand when he wrote the words:

> When I survey the wondrous cross
>   on which the Prince of Glory died,
> my richest gain I count but loss,
>   and pour contempt on all my pride.
> Were the whole realm of nature mine,
>   that were an offering far too small;
> love so amazing, so divine, demands my soul, my
>   life, my all.

(*The United Methodist Hymnal,* No. 298)

8

The Place Jesus Has Prepared for Us

ETERNAL LIFE Made Known

"I HAVE PREPARED YOU A PLACE"

*D*o not let your hearts be troubled. Believe in God, believe also in me. In my Father's house there are many dwelling places. If it were not so, would I have told you that I go to prepare a place for you? And if I go and prepare a place for you, I will come again and will take you to myself, so that where I am, there you may be also. And you know the way to the place where I am going." Thomas said to him, "Lord, we do not know where you are going. How can we know the way?" Jesus said to him, "I am the way, and the truth, and the life. No one comes to the Father except through me." (John 14:1-6 NRSV)

It was an early morning flight out of the Dallas–Fort Worth Airport. The sun had not made its appearance. I was leaving the Council of Bishops meeting early because of two calls. One informed me that my administrative assistant for six years had died of a heart attack. Charles Duke was more than an administrative assistant, he was my friend. I was scheduled a few hours later to deliver the sermon at his resurrection service.

Another call had summoned me to Birmingham because my only sister, Myra, a victim of cancer, was at the point of death. Following Charles's funeral service, I was taking another flight on to Birmingham to say good-bye to her.

You can imagine the state of mind I was in when I boarded the plane to Jackson, Mississippi, and took my aisle seat at the bulkhead. I did not notice when a woman entered and took the window seat. I remained deep within my own thoughts. It was not until the plane began to taxi out to the runway that I noticed my seat partner was crying.

With great reluctance, I placed my hand on her arm and asked if there was something that I could do. She shook her head and turned to face the window. In all honesty, I felt some relief, because I was not in the mood to get involved.

Before the plane became airborne, she turned to me and apologized for her abruptness earlier. Then she asked, "How do you say a final good-bye to someone you love?" She proceeded to tell me that she was flying to Atlanta for the funeral of her life-long friend and college roommate. She talked, nonstop, for more than an hour as we flew. She shared with me that she and her friend had been very close over the years. They shared family vacations and talked to each other by telephone on a weekly basis. She told me how they had directed the weddings of each other's daughters, and later attended the baptisms of grandchildren.

I tried as best I could to reach out to her and let her know that I sensed the deep anguish that she was experiencing. Talking seemed to help. The plane landed in Jackson, and it was not until then, when I began to gather my belongings, that she realized I was deplaning. She seemed stunned and said she assumed everyone was going to Atlanta. At this point, she had not asked me anything about myself—where I lived or what I did for a living.

As I was leaving my seat, she asked me what I was going to do in Jackson. I turned back and said, "I have come to say good-bye to someone I love very dearly, and in a few hours, I will catch another plane to Birmingham to say it again." Time and circumstance of my deplaning did not give me a chance to share more of my story. I am certain she would have been as concerned for my special feelings as I was of hers.

Most of us can identify with this to some degree. It is hard to say good-bye to someone we dearly love. It is an experience that sooner or later invades all of our lives.

This was heavy on the mind and heart of Jesus when he met with his disciples on the evening before his Crucifixion. All of the Gospels relate the deliberate plans and care Jesus gave in the preparation for the meal. He wanted the meal to be a special occasion. He knew that it would be his last time with his friends, and he was to have the sad duty of saying good-bye to them.

In my mind's eye, I can picture his struggling with the knowledge of his coming death and the need to prepare his disciples for it. "How can I possibly explain this to them so that they will understand it," he must have wondered. "How will they handle the pain of my death? How in the world do I say good-bye to my dear friends?"

The truth of the matter is that Jesus tried several times to prepare the disciples. On one occasion he said, "I shall be with you only a little while longer and then I am going to him who sent me" (John 7:33). If the disciples had had ears to hear, they would have understood what Jesus believed about death and eternal life, which would have made his good-bye much easier.

Another day, when he felt the mood of crisis closing in upon him, he said to his disciples, "The hour has come for the Son of Man to be glorified. Truly, truly, I say to you unless a grain of wheat falls into the earth and dies, it remains alone; but if it dies, it bears much fruit" (John 12:23-24 paraphrase). Jesus was saying that what happens to a person in death is much like what happens to a seed when it is planted in the earth. In time, the seed breaks forth into its fullest possibilities of life.

Then, finally, as he sat with them around the meal table, Jesus said, "You must not let yourselves be distressed—you must hold on to your faith in God and to your faith in me. There are many rooms in my Father's House. If there were not, should I have told you that I am going away to prepare a place for you?" (John 14:1-3 Phillips). "I am not going to leave you alone in the world—I am coming to you. In a very little while, the world will see me no more but you will see me, because I am really alive and you will be alive too" (John 14:18-19 Phillips). These words teach us something very important to remember. Saying good-bye is hard! Our emotions don't let us handle it very well, especially when we must say good-bye to someone we really care about. Jesus' words are helpful because he seems to say, "You don't have to say good-bye." Death is not final.

"I go to prepare a place for you, that where I am, you will be also." That is a wonderful gift that Jesus has given to us. The gift of not having to say good-bye.

One can see why the last meal, in the Upper Room, that Jesus shared with his disciples was so important. First of all, he made known something very important about life before death.

Jesus was not the only one who was struggling with saying good-bye. The disciples were anxious about saying good-bye to the world. They were afraid not only for Jesus' life but for their own as well. Jesus seemed to say, "Relax, trust me . . . hold on to your faith in me." Earlier, Jesus had said, "I have come that you might have life in all its fullness." He was making known to them at the Last Supper that he wanted them to live their lives in all their fullness and to look with trust, not fear, to the life that was to come. The New English Bible translates the first verse of John 14, "Set your troubled hearts at rest."

Someone asked Dwight Moody if he had a dying faith. He said, "No! But, I have a living faith, and when it is time for me to die, I'll have a dying faith." This was what Jesus wanted his disciples to understand. Unfortunately, there are well-meaning persons who seem to discount the life that is, in anticipation of the life that is to come.

There is a scene in the last act of Thornton Wilder's play *Our Town* that vividly portrays this problem. Emily, having died at the age of twenty-six, has just arrived at the graveyard of Grovers Corners. The dead townspeople she meets see the living from a different perspective now.

Emily desires to return to her home to relive one day of her life. Although she is warned against it, the "stage manager" gives her permission. She chooses her twelfth birthday to relive. The rules are that she is to live the day just as she had lived it fourteen years earlier.

When Emily comes down for breakfast, her mother is in the kitchen, preoccupied with preparations for the birthday celebration. Her father has just returned from a trip. Only Emily is aware of the few precious moments allowed.

She confronts her mother, ''Mama, just look at me one minute as though you really see me . . . Mama! Fourteen years have gone by, I am dead . . . but for just a moment we are happy. Let us really look at one another.''

No one hears her, for she must relive the day as it was lived before . . . no changes. She can stand it no longer, and cries out, ''I cannot go on. Life goes so fast. We do not take time to look at one another. I never realized all that was going on and we never noticed.''

Emily turns to the ''stage manager'' and asks through her tears to be escorted back to the graveyard. On the way she asks him, ''Do any human beings ever realize how wonderful life is while they are living it?''

That is the crucial question we need to ask ourselves. Ask most people what they believe about the Resurrection and they will answer that it has to do with dying: ''Because Jesus rose from the dead . . . so will I. When I die I will live again.''

What we often fail to understand is that Jesus teaches us that his Resurrection affirms life before death as well as life after death. For the Christian, life is measured by the quality of our life and not the quantity of our years.

When Simon Peter said to Jesus, ''Lord, who else should we go to? Your words have the ring of eternal life!'' he was not saying that Jesus had the keys to just endless life. The Greek word, *aionious*, translated ''eternal'' in this verse, does not mean unending. It means a quality of life other than temporal. Peter was affirming that the eternal life that Jesus offers begins in the here-and-now and is nothing less than the life of God. Jesus not only brought eternal life but is eternal life.

Jesus believed that the continuation of life was so profound that death became a relatively minor matter, like a seed lying dormant in the ground. Death, for him, was an incident, and life was eternal. What if we really believe, as Jesus did, that life is forever? Most people say they believe in immortality, but the way they live denies what they say. What would happen if we could really believe, as Jesus did, that life is eternal?

For many people the questions of life after death are descriptive: where it is and what it is like. There are those who go to great lengths to describe both. Jesus had little to say about it. His promise was that "there is a place prepared and you will be with me." I need no more description. I do not have the slightest idea about what the next world is going to be like, and frankly, this does not bother me. I simply know that one day I will be in the nearer presence and deeper fellowship with God.

I have listened to many different descriptions of what heaven is like. A preacher friend of mine tells about one of these authorities who said, "All the streets are going to be paved in gold, all the walls would have jewels and all the door knobs will be pearl." The friend responded by saying, "Oh, I hope not . . . ," and when he asked why, he responded by saying, "I have lived too long in a parsonage to want pearl door knobs . . . I just want the door knobs to stay on."

We see through a glass darkly now, but one day—whatever heaven is—we will be in the nearer presence of God. This was what Jesus wanted those disciples to know.

The fourteenth chapter of the Gospel according to John reveals Jesus' clear promise of life before and after death. "I am not going to leave you alone in the world—I am coming to you. In a very little while, the world will see me no more but you will see me, because I am really alive and you will be alive too. When that day comes, you will realize that I am in my Father, that you are in me, and I am in you" (John 14:18-20).

The reader must realize that these words were written by John several years after the Crucifixion and Resurrection. However, the words are spoken by Jesus before these events. He was saying, "I am the 'living Christ,' and I will be in your hearts forever." It took Easter for this to become a reality for the disciples. It was not the empty tomb alone that mattered. The mere absence of a body offered no transforming power. If there had been nothing more than this, I doubt if we would have ever heard of Jesus. What changed everything was not the absence of the body but the experience of the "living Christ." This is what Jesus was offering the disciples during their last meal.

What Jesus hoped to hear his disciples testify to that night was what Paul was able to record in his epistle to the Romans: "I have become absolutely convinced that neither death nor life, neither messenger of Heaven nor monarch of earth, neither what happens today nor what may happen tomorrow, neither a power from on high nor a power from below, nor anything else in God's whole world has any power to separate us from the love of God in Christ Jesus our Lord!" (8:38-39). This was what Jesus was seeking to make known among his closest disciples. They were not ready on that night. It would take Easter—its victorious message and joyous meaning—to convince them.

The dawn on Easter brought these same disciples strength out of weakness, affirmation out of disbelief, and the transforming power of God as revealed in a risen Lord. They became witnesses to the Resurrection and to what the power of God can do in the human heart.

Charles Bradlaugh, an avowed atheist who stirred London during the early part of the twentieth century with his attack on the Christian faith, once challenged Hugh Price Hughes, a Methodist preacher who was head of a West End London Mission, to debate the truth of the Christian faith. The preacher accepted readily with one condition. He would bring with him to the debate one hundred men and women who would be witnesses of the redeeming love of God and what it can do in the human heart. They would give evidence and could be cross-examined. They would be persons reclaimed for Christ from brokenness and alienation. They would be witnesses of the transforming power of God in Christ. Hughes asked that his challenger bring a group of persons who had been similarly helped by the gospel of atheism. Needless to say, the debate never came off. The preacher was there with his hundred transformed persons, but Bradlaugh never showed up. And the meeting turned into a testimony time, as redeemed persons bore witness to the power of God in their lives through Christ.

The disciples' lives were transformed because they allowed the living Christ to reign in their hearts. They met him first in Galilee and answered his call to follow him. They lived and labored together for nearly three years. However, it was when they met the "living Christ" following Easter that their lives were changed.

During the Last Supper Jesus made known something very important for us to know about life before death and life after death. However, what he made known about God was his most important revelation at the table.

What kind of God would call us into being, permit us to begin our development as persons and continue it through struggle and effort and pain, and give us glimpses of possibilities beyond; only to let our growth be ruthlessly ended at death, as though it counted for nothing? It is difficult to think that God is like that! Such thinking about God reduces God to an impersonal force without heart.

In the Upper Room that night, around the table, Jesus made known to those disciples—as he had demonstrated so dazzlingly for the three years prior to this evening—that God was not some remote, impersonal force uninvolved in creation. Jesus, who had come to make God's true nature known, demonstrated God's care and compassion by declaring that life was eternal and that a place was prepared for each of them (and us). Just as important was the promise that he would never leave them but would live in their hearts.

John Lincoln Brasher was a pioneer preacher in Alabama. When I joined the North Alabama Annual Conference, he was the oldest living member. He lived to be 103 years of age. I remember him preaching on the one hundredth anniversary of the founding of the conference. He was 102 years of age. He said on one occasion that he had been alive at the death of every member of the conference.

Bishop W. Kenneth Goodson had a wonderful relationship with the old preacher. He tells of the time when he visited Dr. Brasher on the preacher's one-hundredth birthday. The religious news editor of the *Birmingham News* traveled with the bishop to make the visit. Bishop Goodson relates that the rich and wonderful conversation about Dr. Brasher's one hundred years held the reporter spellbound. Finally, it was time to leave.

The bishop said that he could see in the eyes of the young reporter that there was one more question. Then the reporter asked, "Dr. Brasher, how long do you plan to live?"

The old man stood erect, leaning on his ever present staff, and replied, "How long am I going to live? Forever, sir! Forever!"

The next Sunday was Easter. The lead editorial in the *Birmingham News* that Easter Sunday was entitled, "Forever, Sir! Forever!"

I do not understand the mystery. I have no answer for all the hows and whys, but those do not matter. It is enough to be persuaded that "neither death nor life, nor angels nor principalities, nor height nor depth, nor things present nor things to come, nor any other creature shall ever separate us from the love of God which is in Christ Jesus . . ." (Romans 8:38-39 paraphrase).

It is the fundamental question of the Christian faith. I do not know when I am going to die. I only know how long I am going to live . . . Jesus made it known that last night at the table. "Forever, sir! Forever!"

9

Basic Table Manners According to Jesus

HUMILITY Made Known

"THOSE WHO EXALT THEMSELVES WILL BE HUMBLED"

When you are asked by someone to a wedding feast, do not sit down in the place of honour. It may be that some person more distinguished than yourself has been invited; and the host will come and say to you, 'Give this man your seat.'. . . When you receive an invitation, go and sit down in the lowest place, so that when your host comes he will say 'Come up higher, my friend.' Then all your fellow guests will see the respect in which you are held. For everyone who exalts himself will be humbled; and whoever humbles himself will be exalted." (Luke 14:8-11, NEB)

There is an old expression that my father used to describe people who are primarily centered on themselves. The expression was "that person is full of himself." We have all encountered persons who "are full of themselves." If we confess the truth, we, too, have known those moments when we have been "full of ourselves." The sad thing about being full of ourselves is that there is no room for anyone or anything else in our lives. Most assuredly there is no room for God.

Apparently, this was true for many of the religious leaders of Jesus' day. They were so full of themselves that they had no room for any new revelation about God. They busied themselves with unimaginative matters of law.

The Judaism of the Pharisees, with which Jesus was surrounded, seems to have produced a kind of spiritual pride. The piety to which his listeners were accustomed frequently lacked the elements of meekness and modesty. There was an arrogance about the practice of religion. One recalls Jesus' sharp injunction to the disciples, "Beware of practicing your piety before others in order to be seen by them" (Matthew 6:1 NRSV).

Jesus admired the humble spirit. There are numerous sayings and parables throughout the Gospel narratives to communicate his attitude in this respect. The phrase, "for all who exalt themselves will be humbled, and those who humble themselves will be exalted," occurs three times in the Gospel records. In addition, we find this statement: "Whoever becomes humble like this child is the greatest in the kingdom of heaven" (Matthew 18:4 NRSV). A similar statement, "Behold, many of the first shall be last, and the last shall be first," occurs four times. These were evidently habitual phrases with which Jesus kept emphasizing this thought, which he felt so important.

In the Beatitudes one finds, "Blessed are the meek" and "Blessed are the poor in spirit"; in both the quality of humility is praised. And toward the close of the Sermon on the Mount he exhorts people to humility in one of the strongest of all his figures of speech: "Do not judge, so that you may not be judged. For with the judgment you make you will be judged, and the measure you give will be the measure you get. Why do you see the speck in your neighbor's eye? . . . Or how can you say to your neighbor, 'Let me take the speck out of your eye,' while the log is in your own eye? You hypocrite, first take the log out of your own eye, and then you will see clearly to take the speck out of your neighbor's eye" (Matthew 7:1-5 NRSV).

On a sabbath occasion when Jesus was en route to dine in the house of an important leader of the Pharisees, he stopped to heal a man who had dropsy. The Pharisees had been critical of him prior to this for healing on the sabbath and violating other sabbath laws. Jesus asked the lawyers and Pharisees, "Is it lawful to cure people on the sabbath, or not?" But they were silent. So Jesus took the man and healed him, and sent him away. And then he said to the lawyers and Pharisees, "If one of you has a child or an ox that has fallen into a well, will you not immediately pull it out on a sabbath day?" (Luke 14:5 NRSV). They had no reply.

This was typical of the many encounters that Jesus had with the religious leaders. When Jesus spoke of the goodness that was a requisite for entering into the Kingdom, he had to insist that what he meant was not like the religious exclusiveness he observed among the religious leaders. We may conclude that if the religious leaders of the day had not been so self-serving, it would not have been necessary for Jesus to keep insisting on the virtue of a humble spirit.

With this background, consider the events in Luke 14:7-11. Jesus used the occasion to make known his view that the humble spirit is one of life's basic qualities. It was while Jesus dined with a prominent leader that he delivered a lesson in humility.

Jesus was the honored guest for meals on numerous occasions. Hosts were eager to have him in their homes and others were eager to be invited to a banquet where he was present. His notability was generally accepted.

Jesus could not help noticing the positioning and pushing on the part of the guests to occupy the places of honor at the banquet table.

But look through the eyes of Jesus to the caution and reserve of the host and the other invited guests when he entered the banquet room. From the time that Jesus entered the banquet hall, it was obvious that the Pharisees and scribes did not honor the one who was the "honored" guest. He was more of a "curiosity" than anything else.

The Pharisees had other things on their minds. Who would be given the seats of honor at the banquet? Everyone seemed to be maneuvering for seats closest to the host. Much like church members at a covered dish supper, they positioned themselves so they would be at the front of the line or, as in this case, close to one of the honored seats. Some brushed Jesus aside in a frantic effort to position themselves to be recognized and honored. Jesus was the honored guest, but no one seemed to care, not even the host. Jesus had been invited because of his popularity, and they wanted first-hand information about this Galilean rabbi. But that seemed secondary to the personal, not-so-hidden agendas written on their faces.

When the scramble for the best seats was finally over and everyone had reclined at tables, a shocking thing happened. All eyes turned to Jesus who had chosen the least seat.

After observing how the guests had chose the honored places for themselves and had ignored the "honored" guest, he told them the parable of the chief seats.

Jesus not only observed maneuvering among the Pharisees and scribes for prominence and position, but also among his own disciples. James and John sought to occupy the chief seats with Jesus. Jesus reminded them that they were seeking places of honor when in fact the places of honor in his Kingdom were for those who humbled themselves and served others (Mark 10:35-45).

Jesus took the setting of a meal to make known that the humble spirit is one of life's basic qualities.

This was made known in the first place simply because of the innate fineness of Jesus' own spirit. He himself shrank from all ostentation and pretense. Look at every act and deed in the life of Jesus. It was a life of self-denial and humility. The apostle Paul encourages the young Christians to imitate Jesus' example of humility in his letter to the Philippians:

Do nothing from selfish ambition or conceit, but in humility regard others as better than yourselves. Let each of you look not to your own interests, but to the interests of others. Let the same mind be in you that was in Christ Jesus, who, though he was in the form of God, did not regard equality with God as something to be exploited, but emptied himself, taking the form of a slave, being born in human likeness. And being found in human form, he humbled himself and became obedient to the point of death—even death on a cross." (Philippians 2:3-8 NRSV)

The self-assertive attitude of the man in the parable who seized the chief place at the feast was repugnant to the whole disposition of Jesus. His teaching against self-exaltation goes back first of all to this fine quality in his own nature. He could not think in any other terms.

In the second place, Jesus insisted on humility because he thought of goodness as necessarily progressive, and there can be no progress without a humble spirit. A consciousness of one's need to grow is essential. The principle is true in the realm of the intellect as well as that of morals. The person who is sure of his or her own excellence is not likely to hunger and thirst after righteousness. This was one of the lessons that Paul learned in his missionary work, and it accounts for his constantly reiterated exhortation to his converts not to think of themselves more highly than they ought.

This was Jesus' primary conflict with the religious leaders of his day. Jesus was saying to them that God is more than what we ever know. God has more for all of us. For the Pharisee, God's action was all "history." God who spoke was not speaking in their age. Everything was viewed with a backward glance—rituals, feasts, sacrifices.

Jesus said that the goal of life is nothing less than to be perfect, even as God is perfect. With that idea before us, no other attitude is perfect. Before that divine standard, humility is simply honesty with oneself, for in the sight of such an ideal, even the noblest characters recognize their own poverty. When we live in the sight of God and seek his approval instead of the admiration of others, we exemplify the unassuming spirit that we associate with saintliness. The finest spirits are always farthest from self-adulation and self-praise. The reason is that they look forward to the possibilities of life and not backwards to what they have done. In the light of such an ideal, as Jesus set forth, why boast of our slight superiority over our neighbor?

During my last year as pastor of Vestavia Hills United Methodist Church in Birmingham, Dr. Elton Trueblood, eminent scholar, prolific writer of more than thirty books, and vibrant Christian servant, came to preach and teach for several days. He was eighty-three years old. In one of our personal conversations, he shared with me his plans for the future. He said, "Bob, I have learned a great deal through the years as I have studied the Scriptures and fellowshipped with the Lord . . . but I suspect that my most exciting years are ahead . . . ! How about you?"

I do not recall when I have been so touched. He was so vibrant and animated about his faith. He influenced me to surrender any false pride or dependence on the past. I realized that I needed a fresh beginning because my past experience of God can never substitute for my experience of God today.

Someone asked Bishop Kenneth Goodson when he answered the "call" to preach. He responded by asking, "Which one are you talking about, my first call or my last?" He went on to say, "I answered my first call over fifty years ago, when I was a student in Salisbury, North Carolina. The last time was this morning during my morning devotion."

A sure sign of a vital Christian is viability. It comes from genuine humility that finds its origin in an openness to grow and to embrace God's "eternal more"—God's unlimited grace. Vital faith is dynamic, not static.

At 102, Wash Bailey was the oldest living minister and member of the Mississippi Conference until his death in 1991. He had continued to live alone and drive his car. He told me that he would drive "downtown" each morning at ten o'clock. He said, "They sounded the town siren to alert the people to get off the streets." I had noticed that his car looked as though it had been in a demolition derby.

I would visit him from time to time. He stayed current with world events and continued to be keenly interested in the latest developments in the church. He never failed to ask me if I had a church for him to serve. On his one-hundredth birthday, I asked him if he had lived all of his life in Mississippi. He responded, "Not yet!" His excitement about each day and his "not yet" attitude made his life a joy for everyone—but most of all, for himself.

Jesus wanted to make known to those sedentary religious leaders of his day that fellowship with God is an adventure that is never completed. God wants us to be open to new truths about him and new encounters with him in our daily lives. God is never finished with us. These encounters are not always spectacular. There are times when God uses the least expectant moments to get our attention.

It was a beautiful December afternoon. Our three-year-old twin grandsons, Ben and Clint, were spending a few days with us at Lake Junaluska. I accompanied them to a footbridge to feed the ducks. On this particular afternoon, I had been watching a football game on television. But they wanted me to come outside, and I reluctantly joined them.

I was convinced that I could manage them in such a way that I could get back and see the last half. This was not the case. We fed the ducks, skipped rocks on the lake, investigated cloud formations while lying on our backs in the cold grass and experienced myriad wonders that Ben and Clint discovered and pointed out to me on our three-hour excursion. I would never have seen any of it had it not been for Ben and Clint. Most of all, I would have missed the joy of sharing a bit of growing up with my beautiful grandsons.

We can miss the great things God is doing and revealing all around us when we remain full of ourselves. It is possible to be in church and not be there. We can hear the magnificent truths of the gospel and not experience them.

In making his teaching on humility known, Jesus did not demand self-abasement, but offered a challenge of greatness of life. This is why he encouraged his hearers, "Be perfect, therefore, as your heavenly Father is perfect." Then he said, "Blessed are the meek." Christian humility is based on aspiration rather than despair—aspiration combined with honesty. Our eyes look ahead. A humble Christian does not say, "I abase myself," but rather with Paul, "I have not yet apprehended." It is the way to a deep, true self-respect.

There is a small body of water that lies in the southern portion of Russia called the Sea of Azov. Known for its fine sailing waters, there people may sail a boat to their hearts' content. However, if they desire broader waters it is necessary to navigate their sailing craft through the narrow Kerch Strait to reach the larger Black Sea.

If a wider expanse of water is desired, the sailor will need to navigate through the narrow Bosphorus Straits that lead to the Mediterranean Sea. If there still remains a desire for waters more vast than the Mediterranean, then the sailing craft will need to be steered through the Strait of Gibraltar into the extensive waters of the

Atlantic Ocean. If even greater waters are sought, then the boat will need to sail around the treacherous Cape Horn or be navigated through the narrow lakes and locks of the Panama Canal that lead to the largest body of water on earth, the Pacific Ocean.

Jesus was saying to the religious leaders of his day and his disciples, ''God is more than what ever we know of him . . . God has 'more' for us than any of us ever claim.''

10
Interrupted Supper

His COMPASSION Made Known

JESUS WEEPS WITH THOSE WHO WEEP

O *ne of the Pharisees asked Jesus to eat with him, and he went into the Pharisee's house and took his place at the table. And a woman in the city, who was a sinner, having learned that he was eating in the Pharisee's house, brought an alabaster jar of ointment. She stood behind him at his feet, weeping, and began to bathe his feet with her tears and to dry them with her hair. Then she continued kissing his feet and anointing them with the ointment. Now when the Pharisee who had invited him saw it, he said to himself, "If this man were a prophet, he would have known who and what kind of woman this is who is touching him—that she is a sinner." Jesus spoke up and said to him, "Simon, I have something to say to you." "Teacher," he replied, "speak." "A certain creditor had two debtors; one owed five hundred denarii, and the other fifty. When they could not pay, he canceled the debts for both of them. Now which of them will love him more?" Simon answered, "I suppose the one for whom he canceled the greater debt." And Jesus said to him, "You have judged rightly." Then turning toward the woman, he said to Simon, "Do you see this woman? I entered your house; you gave me no water for my feet, but she has bathed my feet with her tears and dried them with her hair. You gave me no kiss, but from the time I came in she has not stopped kissing my feet. You did not anoint my head with oil, but she has anointed my feet with ointment. Therefore, I tell you, her sins, which were many, have been forgiven; hence she has shown great love. But the one to whom little is forgiven, loves little." Then he said to her, "Your sins are forgiven." But those who were at the table with him began to say among themselves, "Who is this who even forgives sins?" And he said to the woman, "Your faith has saved you; go in peace." (Luke 7:36-50 NRSV)*

Luke records an occasion when Jesus was invited as a guest in the home of a Pharisee named Simon. This does not seem to be too uncommon. Those who invited Jesus had their own agenda. It brought them both religious and social notability.

It has been mentioned before that the setting for a formal meal was a three-sided table known as a triclinium. The guests reclined on the outer sides, resting on their elbows with feet outstretched. There were usually cushions distributed around the wall for others who might wander in to hear the noted guest. These persons might be friends, neighbors, or any other curious inquirer who was not invited for the meal but drifted in and out during the course of the evening. The more who attended, the more complimented was the host.

While the guests were enjoying their meal, a woman of questionable reputation interrupted Jesus' meal. The woman knelt where Jesus was reclining and "wet his feet with her tears and wiped them with her hair."

This story reveals a great deal about the scribes and Pharisees. Simon represents the mentality of the religious community, an attitude of hard-nosed legalism with very little compassion. This is made known in the host's neglect of Jesus, as well as the woman.

Jesus' words to Simon are in response to the fact that he had been treated with less courtesy than other guests. Customs of that time provided for at least three courtesies to be offered to a guest. First of all, the host would greet the guest with a kiss. The second custom was to remove the sandals and provide a servant to bathe the feet of each guest. Then an oil with a pleasant fragrance was placed on the guest's head.

Simon ignored all of these customary practices when Jesus came to his home. Perhaps this was more of an oversight than an overt act designed to embarrass Jesus. Self-righteousness displayed by one's smug, judgmental, and critical nature can subtly slip out. The Simons of the world cannot see their own need for mercy and forgiveness because they are consumed by the shortcomings of others.

Although this attitude receives Jesus' attention, the foremost player in the story is not Simon but the woman.

In the story, the woman reveals a great deal about those who were forgotten and forsaken by society. Unfortunately, there have been

110

those who have tried to give her a name. There are those who insist that she is Mary Magdalene. There is no evidence to support this conclusion. The woman in Luke's account, regardless of her true identity, was symbolic of the many sinners and outsiders for whom the scribes and Pharisees had more scorn than compassion.

It was the custom during this time for women to carry a "tear cup" containing their collected tears. Recent archaeological discoveries have confirmed that these "tear cups" were placed alongside their bodies in the burial tombs. I have seen several that have been uncovered. The vases seem to be small tear-shaped flasks. The women used the container to collect their tears. Normally, it was worn around their necks. When they cried, they placed the tear cup just below the tear duct in order to catch the tears. First one eye and then the other. This was the way they saved their tears.

Picture this woman. The alabaster jar in one hand and the tear cup in the other. With these she attends Jesus. Mingling the perfume with her tears, she unbinds her long hair and dries his feet with her hair as she kisses them.

This was no insignificant thing she did. For a woman to unbind her hair in public was unthinkable. However, she was so overcome with emotion and adoration that she did not stop to think of the appearance of her actions. It was a stunning outpouring of devotion.

What about Jesus would motivate her to behave in such an extreme way? Likely, it was his reputation for reaching out to those heretofore considered outcasts. While sinners in general and tax collectors in particular were numbered among the outsiders, women were also treated as an underclass. This surely attracted the woman to Jesus. No doubt, she believed that Jesus would not reject her.

It is worth noting that Luke records, "Not long after this incident, Jesus went through every town and village preaching and telling people the good news of the kingdom of God. He was accompanied by the twelve and some women who had been cured of evil spirits and illnesses" (Luke 8:1-2). Then Luke goes on to list the names of some of the women who joined the company of the disciples. According to Josephus, the Jewish historian, there was no precedent for what Jesus did. His reputation for including and giving equal treatment to all people spread throughout the land.

While the story gives insight into the self righteousness of Simon the Pharisee and the genuine repentance of the woman, Luke reveals something very special through Jesus.

First of all the God of Jesus cries!

There were several philosophies of life forming during the time of Jesus and the early years of the Christian church. None of these were more influential than Stoicism. The foundation of Stoicism was based on emotional insulation. The motive for helping a neighbor must be from a sense of duty not love. This was the way stoics insulated themselves from pain. Greek and Roman gods were emotionless. Aloofness will get you through.

Jesus' compassion and sensitivity for the woman and for all those he encountered introduces a new dimension about God.

There are at least three occasions recorded in the Gospel accounts when Jesus cries. One of the first times was when he saw Mary and Martha weeping over their dead brother. John records that "Jesus wept." He was identifying with their grief and sorrow.

Another occasion when Jesus cried was when he looked out over the city of Jerusalem, a society troubled and divided. Luke records that when Jesus thought of the future heartache for the people of the city, he was moved to tears.

Located on the Mount of Olives is a lovely chapel erected not far from where tradition claims Jesus cried over the city. The little church is named Dominus Flavid, meaning "The Lord Wept Church." The church is shaped in the form of a tear. On each corner of the building there is a replica of the tear cup. Looking out the window, located above the chapel altar, the worshiper has the same view of the city of Jerusalem that Jesus had the night he wept.

The third occasion when Jesus shed tears was in the Garden of Gethsemane on the night he was betrayed. All three of the Synoptics record the incident when Jesus entered the Garden of Gethsemane to pray. It was following the Last Supper with the disciples. He told his disciples that "My heart is breaking with a death like grief and agony.'' He flung himself on the ground, praying that if it were possible, that the hour might pass him by. Jesus said, "Let this cup pass from me . . .''

There are those who believe that Jesus was talking about "the cup of fate," or "the cup of judgment.'' James Fleming suggests that it was "the cup of tears," the grief and sorrow of the moment that Jesus was asking God to take from him. "The amount of sorrow is more than I can bear. Let this cup pass. . . .''

Another church is located in the Garden of Gethsemane. It is known as the Basilica of the Agony. The altar in this church is supported by a huge cup symbolizing Jesus' cup of sorrow. The word *Gethsemane* means "the place of the olive press.'' The place where Jesus prayed on the Mount of Olives was near an olive press. Olives are pressed by huge stones grinding together to produce oil from the olives. The image provides a dramatic description of what went on in our Lord's heart that night in the garden. He, too, was as one who was pressed down—with grief—producing tears of sorrow.

Not only did Jesus reveal that the God of Jesus cries, but he also demonstrated that God cries when we cry. Because Jesus was one who cried with compassion and sensitivity for the lonely and the disenfranchised, the woman in Luke's story was unafraid to throw herself at Jesus' feet and pour out her tears.

The crucial idea Jesus wanted to make known to his disciples and all of those who choose to follow him is that God calls the faithful to cry when others cry.

The missionary couple had served four years. He was a physician and his wife was a nurse. Daily they opened their primitive clinic, and after a period of time, people of the village and surrounding villages came to trust the missionaries and would come for medical treatments. The lines were long and the hours tedious. When they arrived in Africa, they had one child, aged two and one half. Two years after their arrival in Africa a second child, Mark, was born.

While there was active support from the villagers for the medical treatment given in the clinic, no one attended the worship services on Sunday. Faithfully, the missionary couple and their children would conduct Sunday worship. The missionary doctor and his wife would take turns preaching and teaching, as well as playing the little pump organ. For four years, they worshiped in this way. Never did any villager attend a worship service.

After four years in Africa, when Mark was two, he became critically ill. The missionary doctor knew the hopelessness of the illness. In a few days little Mark died. The broken-hearted couple went to the primitive chapel and conducted a worship service. No one from the village attended the funeral.

Afterwards, the father rolled the little boy up in a quilt and carried him out to the edge of the bush. He dug a crude grave. While no one attended the funeral, the couple was keenly aware that the village people had watched closely, from a safe distance, the entire proceedings since the child's death.

When the grave was finished and just before the grief stricken father placed his baby son in the grave, the missionary could stand it no longer and broke down and wept. He wept long and hard. The tears seemed unending.

The next day was Sunday. Faithfully, the missionary family made their way to the chapel for Sunday services. When they arrived, hundreds of villagers had gathered under the arbor. When the missionary asked the old chief to explain why the people had come to worship after all these years, the chief answered, "Yesterday we discovered that you cry like we cry."

What a beautiful aspect of the nature of God that Jesus makes known in Luke. The God of Jesus cries like we cry—and cries when we cry. He, in turn, calls us to cry when others cry. People will know the compassion of Jesus when they see his compassion lived out in our lives.

While they might not have admitted it, there was a deep sense of stoicism among the Pharisees and other religious leaders of Jesus' day. They repressed all emotion. They were impassive in the face of all joy and grief. To express one's grief through tears was a sign of weakness.

Jesus corrected this misunderstanding of God. Jesus has made it known that God cares and cries with us.

11
Called to Be the Life of the Party

His HUMOR Made Known

JESUS LAUGHS WITH THOSE WHO LAUGH

*T*hen Levi gave a great banquet for him in his house; and there was a large crowd of tax collectors and others sitting at the table with them. The Pharisees and their scribes were complaining to his disciples, saying, "Why do you eat and drink with tax collectors and sinners?" Jesus answered, "Those who are well have no need of a physician, but those who are sick; I have come to call not the righteous but sinners to repentance."

Then they said to him, "John's disciples, like the disciples of the Pharisees, frequently fast and pray, but your disciples eat and drink." Jesus said to them, "You cannot make wedding guests fast while the bridegroom is with them, can you? The days will come when the bridegroom will be taken away from them, and then they will fast in those days." He also told them a parable: "No one tears a piece from a new garment and sews it on an old garment; otherwise the new will be torn, and the piece from the new will not match the old. And no one puts new wine into old wineskins; otherwise the new wine will burst the skins and will be spilled, and the skins will be destroyed. But new wine must be put into fresh wineskins. And no one after drinking old wine desires new wine, but says, 'The old is good.'" (Luke 5:29-39 NRSV)

Christians have a difficult time recognizing the humor in the life of Jesus. How many paintings or drawings of Jesus have you seen of him laughing or smiling? Can you recall any works of art that portray Jesus as enjoying himself and others? We tend to see him as the "man of sorrows" and not the "man of joys."

When our youngest son was a preschooler, I was reading to him one night from the Bible for our devotion. I read that portion of the Sermon on the Mount when Jesus spoke of the importance of removing the log from your own eye before bothering with the speck that is in your neighbor's eye. He laughed because he saw, as a five year old, how preposterous it would be for a person to be so deeply concerned about a speck in another person's eye, that he was unconscious of the fact that his own eye had a beam in it. Because the idea of having a log in a human eye was so ludicrous, even to a five year old, he laughed.

I must confess that his laughter stunned me. I was not expecting this sensitive reaction. However, it made me more attentive to the humor in all aspects of Jesus' teaching. Jesus' humor is not always apparent. Sometimes the teachings must be read and reread to catch it.

Nowhere is Jesus' humor more evident than when he exposed pompous people whose acclaim to goodness far exceeded their practice. Vanity is a great weakness of humankind in general, but it seems especially ludicrous when it appears among the religious leadership. The contradiction between human smallness before God and our strutting before others is a perfect opening for ridicule, and Jesus employed it to perfection. His humor was never vindictive but crisp enough to jolt the braggart.

A contemporary example of this art is illustrated by an occasion when a minister said to his wife, "You know dear," in a very pious tone, "there are only a few great preachers left . . ." And she replied, "Yes, and there is one less than you think."

We make a mistake if, in studying the Gospels and watching for evidence of humor, we look only for that which brings full laughter. Frequently there is only a slight touch of humor, such as we find in Jesus' words about the religious leaders, "They go through life with their eyes open, but see nothing, and with their ears open, but understand nothing of what they hear" (Matthew 13:13). Often the smile comes because Jesus reveals to us some of the absurdity of our own lives, where we need help to recognize it.

It is very important to understand that the evident purpose of Christ's humor is to clarify and increase understanding, rather than to hurt or embarrass. The attack may be strong when the object is the

Pharisaic spirit, but it isn't an attack upon an individual Pharisee.

Perhaps the greatest difference between Christ's humor and ours is the use of the humorous anecdote for its own sake. The laugh for which we strive is often the sole justification of the entire effort. We seek humor for humor's sake. This approach is illustrated when a member of an altar guild was attending to the pulpit after the morning service. She noted that the pastor had left his sermon notes on the pulpit. She read, scribbled in pencil on the margin, these words, "use funny story in this place . . . sermon material weak." With Jesus, however, the purpose is always the revelation of some facet of truth that would not otherwise be realized. The humor of Jesus is utilized, it would appear, only because it is a means of calling attention to what would remain hidden or unappreciated without it. Truth, and truth alone, is the end.

That Christ associated with the "laughing people," including what the New English Bible calls "many bad characters," was extremely shocking to the religious leaders. Could there be any depth to Jesus' teaching if he failed to see how unworthy these laughing people were? "Now the tax collectors and sinners were all drawing near to them. And the Pharisees and the scribes murmured, saying, 'This man receives sinners and eats with them' " (Luke 15:1-2 paraphrase).

Part of Jesus' appeal to the outcasts was not only his willingness to eat with them, but also a willingness to laugh with them. Jesus did not fit the expected pattern. Those who gathered around John the Baptist, like those who followed the Pharisaic party, engaged in solemn fasts, but Christ did not do so. Both he and his disciples were notorious for their feasting (Luke 5:33). Though only his enemies called him a drunkard and a glutton, it is obvious that Jesus enjoyed the company of others at feasts, and more important to note, others enjoyed his company, thus his many invitations to dine.

One of his most humorous rejoinders, used to point out that his critics could not be pleased, prompted his invitation for supper by a Pharisee. If people did not like the seriousness of John, and if they also did not like the gaiety of Jesus, what did they want?

"What can I say that the men of this generation are like—what sort of men are they? They are like children sitting in the marketplace calling out to each other, 'We played at weddings for you, but you wouldn't dance, and we played at funerals for you, but you wouldn't cry!' For John the Baptist came in the strictest austerity and you say he is crazy. Then the Son of Man came, enjoying food and drink, and you say, 'Look, a drunkard and a glutton, a bosom-friend of the tax-collector and the outsider!' So wisdom is proved right by all her children!'' (Luke 7:31-35 paraphrase).

The sharp thrust of this final line is characteristic of Christ's sly humor. He is willing to rest the case in terms of human consequences. No one could hear his rejoinder without being amused. Surely, some of the more stoic Pharisees could not, or would not, see the humor, but there must have been others who were amused. At least the Pharisee who invited him to his home for dinner wanted to hear more.

That humor and compassion are compatible is one of the greatest lessons we can learn. Abraham Lincoln often eased tensions in his cabinet by incorporating healthy humor into the most serious moments. It helped him to carry the burdens of the dark days of the American Civil War. Artemus Ward was Lincoln's favorite author. He was a newspaper man who wrote humorous prose. Lincoln was one of Ward's favorite targets.

In *Abraham Lincoln—The War Years,* Carl Sandburg shares some recorded words of Edward Staunton, Lincoln's Secretary of War. According to Sandburg, Staunton records that on September 22, 1862, the cabinet was summoned to the president's office. When they entered, President Lincoln was reading and laughing. "Gentlemen, have you ever read any of Artemus Ward?" he asked them. He then proceeded to read a chapter from the book. It was a spoof on preachers, another favorite target of Artemus Ward.

Staunton wrote that Lincoln was convulsed in laughter as he read from the book while the cabinet sat in all seriousness. Then Lincoln put the book down, sighed deeply, and said, "Gentlemen, why don't you laugh? With the fearful strain that is upon me night and day . . . if I did not laugh I should die, and you need the medicine as much as I.''

I have been fascinated by the story of Norman Cousins, who in a little book entitled *Anatomy of an Illness,* tells how he "laughed his way to recovery." Cousins was diagnosed as having a serious illness. After several weeks of hospital confinement and with little progress toward recovery, he asked his doctors to allow him to treat his own case. This is what he asked to do. First of all he asked that he be permitted to move out of the hospital into a motel across the street. Secondly, that all drugs other than doses of Vitamin C be discontinued, and finally, that he be allowed to view films and videos of comedies. All of his wishes were granted. He was cured. Norman Cousins was convinced that laughter is responsible for his recovery.

Far from laughter being incompatible with anguish, it is often the natural expression of deep pain. Søren Kierkegaard echoed this conclusion when he said that the comic and the tragic touch each other at the absolute point of infinity.

Any form of Christianity that fails to express itself in joy, at some point, is clearly unauthentic. Christians are joyful, not because they are blind to injustice and suffering, but because they are convinced that these, in the light of divine sovereignty, are never ultimate. The humor of the Christian is not a way of denying tears, but rather a way of affirming something that is deeper than tears.

If Christ laughed a great deal, as the evidence shows, and if he is what he claimed to be, we cannot avoid the logical conclusion that there is laughter and gaiety in the heart of God. The deepest conviction of all Christian theology is the affirmation that the God of all the world is like Jesus Christ. If we take this seriously, we conclude that God cannot be cruel, self-centered, vindictive, or even lacking in humor. The God of Jesus laughs! Just as the stoic-minded Pharisees had difficulty with the tears of Jesus, revealing a God who cries, they found difficulty with his laughter.

Though the battle Jesus waged was on two fronts, one of these occupied far more time and effort than did the other. This was the front against the religious opposition, represented primarily by the opposition of the Pharisees. It is here that the strategy of laughter was more appropriate and effective than on the political front, for bigotry is peculiarly vulnerable to ridicule. Jesus' most vocal enemies were those who saw, in him and his teaching, a threat to their own religious program. It was Pascal who—in his notes on morality and doctrine in *Pensées*—said, "Men never do evil so completely and cheerfully as when they do it from religious conviction."

Jesus' major weapon against the Pharisaic attack was laughter, and he used it fully. The point at which they were most vulnerable was their manifest self-righteousness. There is no doubt that, in one way, the Pharisees were good men. They saw the evils of looseness, and the best of them made a great effort to be consistent in practicing the law. They agreed with Jesus that the way is narrow, and they sincerely tried to follow it. They were intentionally pious and sought, without compromise, to keep rigorously to the laws of Moses.

The Pharisees exhibited an undoubted dedication, which is always a source of power, though it is not always a power for good. It was the great merit of the Pharisees that they tried to take their religion seriously. They sought to make, not a mere gesture, but a real effort to attain righteousness. In short, they were perfectionists. Their great mistake, however, was the supposition that, because they adhered so rigorously to the rule of perfection, they had actually attained it.

On one occasion when Jesus was dining in the home of Matthew, he makes first use of the parable. He uses it in response to a question why his followers acted so differently from the followers of John the Baptizer and the Pharisees. Specifically, it was noted that Jesus and his followers seemed to enjoy life. Because the contrast was shocking, the desire for explanation was undoubtedly sincere. The novelty was such that the people simply did not understand. In order to make understanding possible, and while sitting around the supper table, Christ told the double parable of the patched cloth and of the new wineskins.

Jesus makes known the need for radical change by referring to patched garments and to leather containers of wine. If the fresh, or unshrunk, section of cloth is put on the old and shrunken cloth of the used garment, it will pull away the stitching as it shrinks, and the hole will eventually be bigger than it was before. The imagery of shrunken patches and gaping holes in the garment is meant to be amusing. The message is that Jesus was not patching up the imperfect Pharisaism, but was instead instituting something really new.

The example of the wineskins makes the same point in a slightly different form. Wine was contained in the skins of animals, such as goats, and these, for a while, served their purpose well. When the skins were fully sealed, they were efficient containers. But the day came, of course, when the skins were old and dried out and therefore more vulnerable to pressure from within, especially at the forming cracks. If, in such old skins, new wine was poured, the result would be disastrous, said Jesus. This was because the still fermenting new wine would expand and thus bring too much pressure on the old, hard, inflexible container. Then it was a foregone conclusion that the skins would burst, and both containers and wine would be lost.

The obvious teaching is that a system like that of the Pharisees is so inflexible that it cannot contain the new fermenting wine of the spirit that is appearing. The systems of fasts cannot be reformed; it has to be abandoned and new containers must be found.

Luke adds a revealing sentence that is a wonderful example of Jesus' sly humor, in spite of the obvious tendency to make all things as serious as possible. "Of course, nobody who has been drinking old wine will want the new at once. He is sure to say, 'The old is a good and sound wine.' "

We can be grateful to Luke for keeping this delightful touch, which, apart from him, we should never have known. It is the real punch line of the parable, but unfortunately, often goes unnoticed. When it is noticed, there is often a failure to laugh, because some people actually conclude that Jesus is arguing that the old ways are better. Once we rid ourselves of the false notion that Jesus is always deadly serious, it is not very hard to see what he meant. He says there must be a new start, that the old methods will not contain the new life that is emerging, but we must never delude ourselves that most people will like it this way. Most people will say, "We never did it that way, we always did it another way,'' and they will believe, in their innocence, that what they are using is a clinching argument. Many will arise to say, "The old wineskins were good enough in my childhood, and for my mother and father, so they are good enough now.''

In any case, we know that people like the familiar; they tend to resist change, even when the old ways are clearly failing. How good to know that Christ understood this, and that he explained it so slyly and humorously, without undue emphasis. Whether the disciples smiled or not, we do not know, but we know he brings a smile to us now.

This is a wonderful example of Jesus' humor. It is a humor that sharpens the point of the parable, which Jesus had already made. Jesus never used a corny anecdote for the sake of being humorous. The humor comes in quietly, as an extra dividend that we do not expect.

At Matthew's dinner table, Jesus made known that faith is dynamic, not static. Communion with God is an adventure that is never completed. He wanted those first listeners and all who would be his followers to be open and receptive to new truths about him and fresh encounters with him in our daily life. He is never finished with us; therefore, we never finish growing. Whatever has happened to us, it is only the beginning to what God is about to do. He has much more for all of us.

Once Jesus takes up residence in our hearts, a dynamic process begins by which everything is made new. The miracle of the new creation begins. The old person in us is made into a new person. We become new creatures in Christ.

Laughing was as much a part of living as crying for Jesus . Both were vital emotions in his life. He had a difficult time with deadness in persons, which rendered them incapable of either passionate joy or agonizing sorrow. When Jesus offers us life, he offers it ''more abundantly'' than anything we have ever known. Of all the gifts that God has to offer us in life, none is more splendid than his life-giving joy.

Years ago, when Methodist preachers were housed in the homes of families during the annual conference, an elderly widow requested that three ministerial delegates be assigned to her home. Her only request was that she be given pastors who enjoyed life and had a sense of humor. One of the three pastors assigned to the widow's home, affectionately called an "old-stick-in-the-mud" by one of the other pastors, did not measure up to the woman's request.

Each night when they returned from the meetings, the dear woman had cookies and lemonade waiting for them. She would sit around the kitchen table with them and listen to their "preacher yarns." They laughed into the early hours of the morning—that is, all except the "old-stick-in-the-mud." He sat through it all without cracking a smile.

One of the night sessions lasted longer than the others. The widow announced it was time for all to retire for the evening for fear their boisterous laughter should disturb the neighbors. The serious pastor said, in a pious voice, "Before we retire, let us go to the Lord in prayer." To which the hostess responded, "I think not! If you have not felt God's presence in the warmth of our laughter and joy, I do not believe that prayer will help you do so. Good night, gentlemen." And with that she went to bed.

In his winsome and humorous way, Jesus is saying we need a new garment, not a patched old one. We cannot patch up our old self with a fragment of the gospel. The old wineskins cannot contain the new work that Jesus is creating in our lives. Whatever has been my experience of God in the past cannot substitute for the experience of God today. May our prayer be, "Lord, here is a fresh wineskin . . . fill me."

12

More Than Bread and Wine

The NEW COVENANT Made Known

"HE WHO HAS DIPPED HAND IN THE DISH WITH ME,
WILL BETRAY ME"

*T*hen came the day of Unleavened Bread, on which the Passover lamb had to be sacrificed. So Jesus sent Peter and John, saying, "Go and prepare the Passover meal for us that we may eat it." They asked him, "Where do you want us to make preparations for it?" "Listen," he said to them, "when you have entered the city, a man carrying a jar of water will meet you; follow him into the house he enters and say to the owner of the house, 'The teacher asks you, "Where is the guest room, where I may eat the Passover with my disciples?" ' He will show you a large room upstairs, already furnished. Make preparations for us there." So they went and found everything as he had told them; and they prepared the Passover meal.

When the hour came, he took his place at the table, and the apostles with him. He said to them, "I have eagerly desired to eat this Passover with you before I suffer; for I tell you, I will not eat it until it is fulfilled in the kingdom of God." Then he took a cup, and after giving thanks he said, "Take this and divide it among yourselves; for I tell you that from now on I will not drink of the fruit of the vine until the kingdom of God comes." Then he took a loaf of bread, and when he had given thanks, he broke it and gave it to them, saying, "This is my body, which is given for you. Do this in remembrance of me." And he did the same with the cup after supper, saying, "This cup that is poured out for you is the new covenant in my blood." (Luke 22:7-20 NRSV)

Unlike the other meals where Jesus is a guest, the Last Supper was hosted by Jesus himself. Whereas in most of the other occasions Pharisees, scribes, Sadducees, and people from off the street made up the guests and spectators, this meal is exclusively for the Twelve.

Luke records that Jesus dispatched Peter and John to make the necessary arrangements. This included securing the place and making preparations for the meal. The place had been reserved by Jesus, and he gave the disciples directions to meet a man who was to lead them to a house with a furnished upper room.

So on his last evening, Jesus gathered his disciples together to eat the Passover meal. Only ceremonial meals were eaten at the beginning of the night. The customary hour for the main meal was earlier in the afternoon.

"When the time came, he took his seat at the table with the apostles, and spoke to them,

" 'With all my heart I have longed to eat this Passover with you before the time comes for me to suffer. Believe me, I shall not eat the Passover again until all that it means is fulfilled in the kingdom of God' " (Luke 22:14-16).

During the supper Jesus took a flat, round loaf of bread, broke it, as was the custom, and divided the portions of the one loaf among his disciples. In the same way after supper, he passed a cup of wine among them and each disciple drank from it.

Anyone of the ancient world would have understood the meaning of such an act without explanation. The disciples had been a close knit group over the preceding three years. At the end of each day, they sat at table together to refresh themselves and share their stories. Now Jesus wanted them to feel a renewed unity. For eating together binds the partakers of the meal to one another.

Jesus was preparing them to remain united during his upcoming separation from them, until the day when the table of unity is renewed in the Kingdom of God.

After supper two items of conversation prevailed. First, in response to Jesus' statement that the one who would betray him was with them, they began to ask which one of them it could be. Then a dispute arose among them as to who should rank highest and be regarded as greatest. This discussion had been on their lips when they entered the Upper Room. Several things had ignited the issue during the day, including the actions of the ambitious mother of James and John who lobbied for her sons places of prominence (Matthew

20:20-28). This dispute had continued even while the disciples took their places at the table.

Jesus announced that one of the disciples would betray him. When the disciples inquired as to whom he could mean, Jesus answered, " 'It is the one I am going to give this piece of bread to, after I have dipped it in the dish.' Then he took a piece of bread, dipped it in the dish and gave it to Simon's son, Judas Iscariot" (John 13:26-27).

The custom of dipping in a common bowl and feeding those reclining nearby was the practice at the Passover meal. Several bowls were distributed around the tables. Normally, three or four persons shared a bowl. If Jesus dipped the bread and gave it to Judas, then Judas must have been at his left. In other words, Jesus chose Judas to sit in the honored place. Jesus, desiring to express love to Judas, invited him to sit next to him at the Last Supper.

The disciples positioning themselves for places of honor as well as a general insensitivity to Jesus are sad preludes to what was to happen in the next few hours.

This was more than the observance of the Passover meal. The basic idea of Passover was the celebration of the Israelites' deliverance from the slavery and bondage of Egypt. Israel firmly believed that, through this action, God had established a covenant with them. They were to be his people. He was to be their God. The laws of God bound them to one another. By obeying God's laws, the people were obedient to God, observing the covenant. In breaking God's laws, the people were disobedient to God, rejecting the covenant.

Israel believed that access to God came by keeping his laws. Sin obstructed their access. Sin kept placing obstacles between God and the people. The whole sacrificial system of the Jews had as its one aim and object the restoration of the relationship between God and the people, which sin kept destroying. What the Gospels are saying in their accounts of the Last Supper is that by the life and death of Jesus, he established a new covenant with God, based not on a relationship of law, but on a relationship of redemptive love. This is confirmed in the prayer of Great Thanksgiving in the Service of Holy Communion:

Almighty God, our heavenly Father, who of thy tender mercy didst give thine only Son Jesus Christ to suffer death upon the cross for our redemption; who made there, by the one offering of himself, a full, perfect, and sufficient sacrifice for the sins of the whole world. . . . (*The Book of Worship* [Nashville: The United Methodist Publishing House, 1964], p. 20.)

In the Upper Room, Jesus says to his disciples, "This cup of the new covenant made in my own blood which is shed for you. See this wine poured into the cup. My blood shall be poured out for you. And as I break this bread, so my body will be broken . . . and it will be for you. All of this is for your sakes . . . because of my love for you."

It was not the celebration of the old covenant symbolized in the ancient feast of the Passover, but was the new covenant that Jesus made known that night in the Upper Room. The apostle Paul acknowledged the significance of the covenant meal when he wrote to the young church at Corinth, "The Lord Jesus, on the night when he was betrayed took a loaf of bread, and when he had given thanks, he broke it and said, 'this is my body that is for you. Do this in remembrance of me.' In the same way he took the cup also, after supper, saying, 'this cup is the new covenant in my blood. Do this, as often as you drink it, in remembrance of me' " (I Corinthians 11:23-25 NRSV).

Breaking bread was a symbol of deep intimacy, unbroken by any separation, marred by no betrayals or forgetfulness. It is difficult for those of us for whom sharing a meal is routine to appreciate the enormity of Judas's treachery, Peter's denial, and the flight of the disciples with frightened faces turned over their shoulders toward the cross. It was the breaking asunder of the holiest covenant one individual could bind with another. Yet even in the face of this Upper Room covenant torn to shreds by the disciples, the new covenant assures all people of an invitation to the new covenant meal where Christ is present amid the breaking of bread.

When we celebrate the sacrament of the Lord's Supper, it is not a reenactment of the Last Supper and a time to focus only upon the defeat and gloom of the cross. If this were true we would have Communion once a year at Maundy Thursday.

Christians have gathered for nineteen hundred years to "break bread" amid suffering, pain, and injustice. They did this and we continue the tradition in order to remember who we are and the victory that is ours in Jesus Christ. When we gather around the table and our lives are encountered by Christ's being, we are changed. We will never be the same. We rise from the table and go away as changed persons better able to live and not just face life.

I have encountered this at the "table" throughout my ministry as a pastor and bishop in the church. I have witnessed persons who have struggled within their families and marriages be reconciled at the "table." Christ was present in our midst, reconciling and making free those who were alienated from others.

There have been special times when persons experiencing separation from loved ones have been comforted at the "table." During times of war, family members have brought their pain and suffering that comes from separation from sons, daughters, fathers, mothers, wives, and husbands. I have met with them at the table in the sanctuary, and we have celebrated the Lord's Supper. It was for them what it was for the first Christians. Their eyes opened, resurrection occurred, and the families were able to rise and share with the world that "He is risen!"

There have been those special times and places far from home when the new covenant has been made known to me. When language was a barrier—in places like Mozambique, Korea, Nicaragua, or Estonia—the presence, the joy, and the love, were present at the "table" as we shared in the breaking of bread.

The special bonding that comes from sharing the covenant meal was made known to me in a powerful way at a council of bishops meeting. It was during the early struggle for independence and self-determination by the countries of eastern Europe. My colleague and friend Ruediger Minor, bishop of the Dresden Area in East Germany, was a primary leader in the struggle. He suffered much for his convictions.

At the same time the struggle for self-determination in Eastern Europe was going on, revolution was taking place in Liberia. Like

Bishop Minor, Bishop Arthur Kulah was courageously negotiating for peace and reconciliation in his west African country. He had to flee the country in the aftermath of the revolution with only the clothes on his back.

When we celebrated the Lord's Supper on the last morning of our meeting, I found myself kneeling between my brothers Ruediger Minor and Arthur Kulah. As we ate the bread and drank from the cup, I felt of one accord with them and their people's struggle.

This is what happens when we gather with our brothers and sisters in Christ, when the bread is broken and blessed, when the bread and wine are given: we joyfully remember that Christ is in our midst. We rejoice in our unity with him and one another. Like the earliest disciple that evening at Emmaus, our "eyes are opened" and we see.

It is no small thing that the "breaking of bread" was the distinctive act of worship of the first believers. It was a continuation of the table covenant that the original disciples had enjoyed with Jesus. Though he was no longer with them in the flesh, they could celebrate together the simple meal at which he had once presided in person. It was a meal that brought back memories of the times when he had broken the bread here on earth. Especially they would recall the Last Supper "on the night he was betrayed." But the spirit in which they partook of the meal was not one of sadness or sorrow. They broke bread "with simple joy" (Acts 2:46). Their eyes were fixed on the banquet of the Kingdom of God. Jesus had promised to drink with them anew at that time.

13
A Second Helping

GRACE Made Known

"ALL IS FORGIVEN...FEED MY SHEEP"

*J*ust after daybreak, Jesus stood on the beach; but the disciples did not know that it was Jesus. Jesus said to them, "Children, you have no fish, have you?" They answered him, "No." He said to them, "Cast the net to the right side of the boat, and you will find some." So they cast it, and now they were not able to haul it in because there were so many fish. That disciple whom Jesus loved said to Peter, "It is the Lord!" When Simon Peter heard that it was the Lord, he put on some clothes, for he was naked, and jumped into the sea. But the other disciples came in the boat, dragging the net full of fish, for they were not far from the land, only about a hundred yards off.

When they had gone ashore, they saw a charcoal fire there, with fish on it, and bread. Jesus said to them, "Bring some of the fish that you have just caught." So Simon Peter went aboard and hauled the net ashore, full of large fish, a hundred fifty-three of them; and though there were so many, the net was not torn. Jesus said to them, "Come and have breakfast." Now none of the disciples dared to ask him, "Who are you?" because they knew it was the Lord. Jesus came and took the bread and gave it to them, and did the same with the fish. This was now the third time that Jesus appeared to the disciples after he was raised from the dead. (John 21:4-14 NRSV)

My mother was the best cook in the world. Most children think that, but mine really was. She made the most wonderful desserts. My favorite was her chocolate cake with mocha icing. When I was a child and no one spoke of metabolism, I was able to eat my weight in "Mimi's Mocha Cake." She would let me scrape the icing bowl and that was the best part.

It was difficult for me when we entertained guests for a meal, and I was allowed only one piece of cake. There were no greater words for my ears to hear than when guests had left and my mother would say, "Bobby, do you want a second helping of cake?" The second helping is the portion that we do not expect or deserve but desperately desire.

The last known meal that Jesus shared with his disciples was recorded only by John. It was a breakfast that Jesus prepared on the shore of the Sea of Galilee.

The memorable scene that serves as a preface to all of the post-Resurrection events is the scene of Jesus and the disciples in the Upper Room on the night Jesus was arrested. The fear and tension were felt by the group. Peter said, with sincere resolve, to Jesus, "Lord, I am ready to go with you to prison and death. Even though the others fall away, I will not." Those are the words that come from a determined disciple.

Peter must have been shattered when Jesus responded to him by saying, "Peter, I tell you, this very night the cock will not crow until you have three times denied that you know me. . . ."

That night the soldiers came and took Jesus away while Peter followed at a "safe" distance in the shadows (John 18:16). He remained that night in Caiaphas's courtyard, warming himself around the fire.

On three separate occasions that night, Peter was identified as a disciple. First by a servant girl who asked, "Are you one of this man's disciples, too?"

"No, I am not," retorted Peter.

A little later someone else said, "Surely you, too, are one of his disciples, aren't you?" Peter again denied it.

Then one of the High Priest's servants remarked, "Didn't I see you in the garden with him?" And again Peter denied it. And immediately the cock crowed.

Luke records that the cock crowed as they were transferring Jesus to another location. Jesus looked at Peter. What a look that must have been. Peter could say nothing. He went out into the night and wept bitterly.

How much would happen before Jesus and Peter were face to face again! Little did Peter realize that by morning Jesus would have been tried and on his way to the cross. Peter's parting with his Master was one of denial and failure. That look was etched in his memory. What a wretched and forlorn feeling. Even the exciting announcement of the empty tomb failed to lift Peter's dejected spirit.

This was the feeling that accompanied Peter and the disciples back to Bethsaida and their fishing boats.

John records that the disciples fished all night and caught nothing. At the first break of light, a wonderful scene takes place. From the beach a stranger called out, "Have you caught anything?" They indicated that they had not. "Throw your net on the right side of the boat," said Jesus, "and you'll have a catch."

So they threw out the net and found that they were not strong enough to pull it in because it was so full of fish! It was at this point that John said to Peter, "It is the Lord!"

When Peter heard this, he left the boat and his friends and swam to shore. Have you ever wondered why? Someone has speculated that he wanted to get to Jesus before the others in order to ask Jesus to forgive him for his denial of him while standing by a charcoal fire in Caiaphas's courtyard. He wanted Jesus to know of his misery and utter sorrow.

My thought is that, amid the excitement of believing this to be Jesus, he wanted to get to him as fast as he could. Somewhere between the boat and shore it must have dawned on Peter, "Will Jesus have anything to say to me? How can I face him after that night. I still remember that look in the courtyard."

When Peter and the other disciples arrived on shore, they discovered that Jesus had made a charcoal fire. Raymond Brown, in his commentary on John's Gospel, makes the point that the Greek term for "charcoal fire" is used only twice in the Bible—once in the courtyard of Caiaphas and once on the Galilean Beach.

Jesus asked for some of the fish they had caught. He added these to the others already on the fire along with some bread. Jesus said to them, "Come and have your breakfast." Jesus took the bread and gave it to them. He then took fish from the fire and served them all fish as well.

This was more than just a friendly gesture on Jesus' part. These disciples knew it. They knew what it meant for someone to invite you to the table. Jesus was making known, in such a beautiful way, his amazing grace. It was as though he could read Peter's mind. Peter was not alone with feelings of guilt and failure. All of the disciples felt the same. They knew they did not deserve the grace that Jesus extended to them.

Now Jesus invites them to the table of reconciliation and grace. It was his way of saying, "It's all right fellows. I know that you regret what you did. But, now let us break bread and eat the reconciliation meal together and then you must follow me and feed my sheep." Jesus' grace enables the sinner to center on the present and the future and not the past.

John opens his account of the gospel with his wonderful affirmation that grace is God's gift from the beginning. Grace is the foundation of our relation with God—that which we take for granted as we live out our lives as Christians. "From his fullness we have all received, grace upon grace" (John 1:16). "And the Word became flesh and dwelt among us, full of grace" (v. 14).

For some strange reason we think of grace as God's gift of love and forgiveness given to us after we struggle through life. In other words, grace is given after we do all we can do. The gospel inverts this idea of grace. John Wesley called this prevenient grace . . . the grace that comes before anything we can do. The gospel is clear that grace is ours from "the beginning." The gospel begins with grace.

Jesus makes this known in his relationship with Peter and the disciples. They could not believe his grace would be so generously bestowed upon them until that morning breakfast in Galilee. The gift was always there but they would not receive it. What a difference it would have made in their lives if they had believed it.

Peter and the other disciples had never really grasped the love and grace of God being revealed before them in Jesus. There had remained enough of their strict Pharisaic training that made it difficult to claim such a wonderful gift.

There are so many points in Peter's life with Jesus that we believe to be pivotal in his life. When Jesus called him away from his fishing nets, Peter readily agreed to follow as a fisher of people. It was a courageous move to leave family and to follow an unknown teacher. The time with Jesus on the Mount of Transfiguration appears to increase Peter's loyalty. Many point to the experience at Caesarea Philippi, when Peter acknowledged Jesus as "The Christ." Still others point to the time in the Upper Room, the night Jesus was arrested, when Peter vowed on that evening to follow him to prison or death.

The breakfast encounter on the shores of the Sea of Galilee was a liberating time for Peter. After this experience Peter's life was different. Perhaps this experience, more than any other, freed Peter and the disciples to be the courageous leaders of the early church.

Peter discovered that accepting the grace made known to him in Jesus and living out of that grace afforded a different kind of life than he had known. He was liberated from the straining, contriving, and often contorted understanding of God that had afflicted his life before.

Peter discovered in his reconciling encounter with Jesus that there are certain freedoms, certain liberations, joys, and privileges that come from accepting God's gift of grace.

The first liberation Peter experienced was his freedom from the pressures of his past.

Jesus called men and women to follow him and simply live out the freedom that was demonstrated so beautifully and dazzlingly in his own life. He did not call them to a new law or a new religion. He called them to be children of his Father in heaven and to live out the grace he exemplified so majestically, himself. His was a freedom to face life without fear, without wallowing in the slavery of what has been.

Peter was a product of a strict legalistic religious law. The rules were clear. He knew when he had violated them, and he had been motivated by guilt more than grace for most of his life. To understand Peter's religious position you need only to read about most of the Pharisees that Jesus confronted. They mirrored Peter's religious position at the time of his commitment to follow Jesus. His ideas and opinions were changed to some degree, but a residue of the old legalism was still present.

Peter discovered that God's grace frees us from the past and gives to us wide vision and great hearts of love and joy. Nowhere is this more evident than in our relationships. God doesn't set us up to keep vigilance on our neighbor's behavior or to monitor their mistakes. For the first time, Peter discovered that God does not call us to be one another's judges and censors. We are to be one another's support and friend.

I have a small painting hanging on my study wall of a pleasant seaside scene with the following caption: "A friend hears the song in my heart . . . and sings it to me when my memory fails."

Relations were made different from anything Peter had ever experienced. For the first time in his life, the joy of liberation enabled him to know true fellowship. This was made possible because he finally knew his worth and that of others—brothers and sisters who are infinitely loved by their heavenly father.

The late Dean Howard Thurman was a pastor, poet, and mystic. This grandson of a slave became an outstanding educator. The chapel on the campus at Rust College in Holly Springs, Mississippi, is named in his honor.

He wrote more than twenty books during his lifetime, and the last was an autobiography entitled *With Head and Heart*. In it he tells how his grandmother, a former slave, used to tell her family about her slave preacher. He never preached a sermon, she remembered, without "going to Calvary." Facing his congregation living under a savage, dignity-denying system, the old preacher would tell them about a just man, unjustly abandoned by God and subjected to humiliation, ridicule, and unspeakable pain. Then he told them how God had raised him from the dead and made him the head of a new world in which they could participate with dignity.

Dean Thurman reports that, according to his grandmother, when the preacher finished telling the story, he would look into the faces of his slave congregation and say, "You are not slaves! You are not 'darkies'! You are God's children."

"When my grandmother got to that part of her story, there would be a slight straightening of her aging back and a stiffening of her jaw, and we forced our chests out a little farther than usual by holding in our breath. When she finished, our spirits were restored," wrote Thurman.

Peter experienced the same when Jesus seemed to say to Peter, "You don't need to bring along the excess baggage of your past. We won't have room for it when we move out to the ends of the earth."

Peter discovered another freedom that morning. Once he claimed God's gift of grace and lived off the power of God's goodness in Christ, he was liberated from anxiety about the future. He was freed from the pressures of the past, and was liberated from the pressures of the future.

Dr. Leslie Weatherhead told of a Methodist circuit rider in England who traveled and preached all across the countryside. There was a time in his life when he experienced much difficulty. At the point of giving up his ministry, he asked God for guidance, but as sometimes happens, it seemed that no guidance came.

One evening, he stopped to eat and sleep in one of the homes of his followers. After supper, he went up to his room where the host had built a fire in the grate. He sat down on the bed and noticed that on the table beside the chair was a Bible opened to Psalm 59. He began to read, and when he came to the tenth verse he found the words, "The God of my mercy shall prevent me" (KJV).

Weatherhead points out that the word *prevent* is a word that has changed its meaning. Nowadays if we prevent someone it means that we stop them from doing something. But when the King James Version of the Bible was produced the word "prevent" meant "to go before." To prevent someone was to go before them. The text really meant, "The God of my mercy shall go before me." But someone else had written their own paraphrase of the verse in the margin. It was just what the circuit rider needed, and he never forgot it. The words written in the margin read, ''My God in His loving kindness, shall meet me at every corner.'' The words were light for his darkened pathway.

The knowledge that God goes before us gives us a sense of assurance. Peter wanted to be brave. He meant what he said to Jesus when he first answered his call. He could not have been more sincere than when he confessed that Jesus was the Christ, or in the Upper Room when he pledged to follow him to death. It was at the reconciling meal that he understood that God's grace was all sufficient.

What a difference it would make in our life if we could believe, amid all the circumstances of life, even when we are afraid and our future seems uncertain, that God is there before us and ''meets us at every corner.''

There is another thing that happened when Peter accepted Jesus' gift of grace. He experienced the freedom from pressures of living in the present. This may have been the most important liberation for Peter.

Peter discovered that the gospel is not a gospel of humiliation but exaltation. The power of God's grace says we do not have to be ashamed. Peter was overwhelmed by God's love, which enfolds and upholds us. Jesus made known to him as they shared that morning meal that Peter could live his life in the assurance of his love and grace. Just as in Peter's case, God does not require our perpetual regret. He sets us free. We cannot recapture the past, but God releases us from the past so that we can live in the now.

Every gesture of our Lord Jesus Christ was filled with a gracious openness to all. He consorted with those whom others said were sinners, outcasts, and degenerates. He was sharply criticized for this, because in representing the grace of God he was not discriminating but lavish in the way he offered God's gift of grace and goodness.

There are persons who might think that Jesus was too easy on Peter. But what good would it have been to have humiliated Peter?

Jesus did not place him on probation. He set him free to be a blessing to the early Christian community.

A story is told about G. Campbell Morgan, who was a great preacher in England some years ago. It was brought to his attention that there was in his community a needy widow with three children. He visited the woman and discovered that she was about to be evicted for failing to pay the rent. That was on a Saturday morning. The next morning, in worship, Morgan told his congregation about the family and received an offering to assist them. Enough money was received to pay all the back rent and several months in advance. The preacher was so excited that he went straight to the woman's apartment following worship. He could hardly wait to tell her the good news. He knocked on the door, but there was no answer. He knocked again, but no one answered, and he went away disappointed. Some time later in the day she got in touch with him. She told him she had been afraid to answer the door, for she thought it was the landlord who had come to collect the rent, when all the time it was a friend bringing her a wonderful gift.

There are so many who picture God as a landlord who comes demanding the rent when in reality Jesus teaches us that God is a friend who brings us a wonderful gift. The gift of his love, his forgiveness, and his grace.

I was struck by the story of the Dutch pastor and his family who during the Second World War joined with others in sheltering Jews from Hitler's forces. They were eventually found out. And one night in the middle of the darkness, they heard the sound of boots and the abrupt knocking at the door. They, along with some of their fellow conspirators, were rounded up and loaded into cattle cars to await the fate of so many of the Jews and those who sheltered them.

All night long, they rode in heart-breaking anguish, jostled against one another, stripped of any form of dignity, knowing only that they were headed for Hitler's extermination centers at Auschwitz, Buchenwald, or Dachau.

After hours of moving alternated with seemingly endless times of standing still, the doors of the cars were opened, and light streamed into that tragic scene. They marched out and were lined up beside the railroad tracks, resigned to unspeakable pain as they knew their families would be split apart.

But in the midst of their gloom, they discovered news that was good beyond belief. They were not in Germany; they were in Switzerland. During the night, someone, through personal daring and courage, had tripped a switch and sent the train to Switzerland. And those who now came to them were not their captors but their liberators. Instead of being marched to death, they were welcomed to life.

The pastor said, in the midst of his joy, "What do you do with such a gift?"

John wrote, "From his fullness we have received grace upon grace" (John 1:16 NRSV). What a marvelous testimony. What a joy to know that this kind of freedom is ours, and to live out of it and to live in it calls us to the most joyful, the most delightful, the most authentic life that God could devise for his children.

Like Peter, may we pray that God will grant in our hearts the kind of basic and fundamental trust in God's goodness and power. May we accept the gift and rely on God's grace, so that we might find new strength and new freedom, both in our personal lives and together as a church.

14
Food to Go

Our MISSION Made Known

"I SEND YOU FORTH...AS MY WITNESSES"

*W*hile staying with them, he ordered them not to leave Jerusalem,
but to wait there for the promise of the Father. "This," he said,
"is what you have heard from me; for John baptized with water,
but you will be baptized with the Holy Spirit not many days from now."
So when they had come together, they asked him, "Lord, is this the time
when you will restore the kingdom to Israel?" He replied, "It is not for you
to know the times or periods that the Father has set by his own authority. But
you will receive power when the Holy Spirit has come upon you; and you will
be my witnesses in Jerusalem, in all Judea and Samaria, and to the ends of
the earth." (Acts 1:4-8 NRSV)

A number of years ago I was invited to deliver the Houston
Preaching Series at the First United Methodist in Concord, North
Carolina. Concord is a lovely community on the outskirts of
Charlotte.

I arrived on the Saturday before I was to preach my first sermon the
next morning. After settling into my room I went over to see the
church. Unfortunately I was not able to get in because it was secured
for the night.

A beautiful stained glass window over the front entrance caught
my attention. The window depicted Jesus standing with his arms
outstretched inviting all to come. A beautiful invitation for the
prospective worshiper. "Come to me all you who are heavy hearted
and I will give you rest." Around the image of Jesus the artist had
included representative persons to whom Jesus had extended the
invitation. There was Zacchaeus; the disciples by the Sea of Galilee;
the woman at the well; Levi, the tax collector; and others. I was

impressed by the appropriateness as well as the beauty of the window.

Several days later, I was standing in the narthex greeting worshipers after one of the worship services. I discovered another feature of the window. There was an open ceiling in the narthex and the window was visible from the inside. Now Jesus seemed to be bidding the worshiper to go. Coming in from the outside the invitation was to come, and leaving the sanctuary the command was to go.

I discovered that the people aptly call the window their "come and go window." I was reminded that Jesus never called anyone to come to him that he did not bid them to go.

At the conclusion of all four Gospels, Jesus makes his mission known to his followers. In Matthew are the familiar words of the "Great Commission," when Jesus said, "You are to go make disciples of all the nations" (Matthew 28:19). In Mark 16:15, "Go out in the whole world and proclaim the gospel to every creature." In John 20:19-21, "Just as the Father sent me, so I am now going to send you."

Luke wrote a two volume commentary. The first being the life of Jesus and the second volume describes the life of the first-century church. At the end of his account of the gospel, he records that Jesus reminds the disciples that they were to be "witnesses of all they had experienced." He further counsels them to stay in Jerusalem, "until you are clothed with power from on high" (Luke 24:48-49).

Luke picks up on this theme in the first chapter of Acts of the Apostles. On an occasion, while Jesus was eating a meal with them, he stressed that they were not to leave Jerusalem, but to wait for the Father's promise. "But you are to be given power when the Holy Spirit has come to you. You will be witnesses to me, not only in Jerusalem, not only throughout Judea, not only in Samaria, but to the very ends of the earth" (Acts 1:8).

Once again, Jesus uses the mealtime to make his mission known to his followers. You are to go out to the whole world witnessing in my name. D. T. Niles reminds us that "the church exists for mission as a fire exists for burning." The Latin root for the word *mission* is *missio*, which means "to go."

Jesus was summoning them to stand up and be counted for the cause, whatever the personal cost might be. They were to go out as "sent persons," emissaries of Christ, envoys of the risen Lord. They were to be preachers of unpopular truth. They were to be witnesses of a crucified Lord. One of the best definitions of what it means to be a witness is that given by Whittaker Chambers in his book *Witness,* where he says,

I will give you an answer: I was a witness. I do not mean a witness for the Government or against Alger Hiss and the others. . . . A man is not primarily a witness *against* something. That is only incidental to the fact that he is a witness *for* something. A witness, in the sense that I am using the word, is a man whose life and faith are so completely one that when the challenge comes to step out and testify for his faith, he does so, disregarding all risks, accepting all consequences. (p. 5)

The main work of Christian discipleship then and now is that of witnessing, not theorizing. The early Christians were not sent out to philosophize about the good life or to discuss academically the latest interpretation and theories. Their witness was simply, "This I know," or "This I have seen," or "This happened to me." Death, torture, imprisonment . . . let them come, as indeed they did to so many of the early Christians! Many of the disciples who heard the Master's words of summons were martyred for their witness. They were sent out to show forth the great facts of the Christian faith. They answered Christ's call and stood up to bear their fair share of the witness to the Christian faith.

The church needs to confess that so much of our emphasis has been on "coming" and not enough on "going." As a result of this emphasis, many people believe that when they "come" they have met all their Christian responsibilities. Unfortunately, for many, church vitality is gauged more on the way we come and not on the way we go into the world.

In John's account of the "Great Commission," Jesus said, "Just as the Father sent me . . . I send you." We are sent out to witness. Someone might ask, "How are we to witness?" The little word *as* is the key. We are to witness "as" Jesus witnessed. As the Father sent Jesus, so now we are sent.

As the Father sent Jesus to witness to the broken world, so he sends us, his followers.

Jesus began his ministry by quoting Isaiah: "The Spirit of the Lord is upon me and he has anointed me to preach good tidings to the poor; He hath sent me to proclaim release to the captives, and recovering of sight to the blind, To set at liberty them that are bruised, to proclaim the acceptable year of the Lord" (Luke 4:18-19).

Jesus' every act was one of loving and caring for the broken and down trodden. His witness was of sustaining those who knew brokenness. There is no record in the Gospels of Jesus condemning anyone. He did not scorn, deride, or disdain anyone—no matter what they had done. His constant invitation was for persons to bring their brokenness to the table of reconciliation. As the Father sent Jesus to witness to a broken world, God also sends all of us who claim to be faithful followers.

There is so much brokenness in our world. Most of the people do not know what to do with their brokenness. We need to confess that often the local church gives unclear signals, thereby making the community church the last place a person will go with their brokenness.

Shortly after my first appointment as pastor, a member came to see me. In the course of the conversation this member shared the brokenness of his life. I saw this person in our congregational worship and activities but never knew the pain deep inside.

After listening for what seemed like hours, I offered a very insensitive cliché. I said, "Why have you waited so long to share this?"

The member's response was, "But, Bob, I know how busy you are with church matters and other people's problems, and I did not want to bother you." The member continued, "Bob, you are so fine and wonderful . . . I just did not want you to know." My member friend thought that was a compliment, but in fact the words ripped at my heart.

Years have come and gone since that encounter, but I continue to keep up with my friend. I have thought many times about those words, "You are so busy . . . and you are so fine and wonderful . . . I did not want to bother you." What have we done in the church to communicate to a broken world that there is not enough time or enough love and understanding in us. The truth hurts. On many occasions we in the church are the first to throw stones.

Many have heard me time and time again say that my prayer is that each congregation will have the reputation in the community for loving the broken. When people are hurting and their life has fallen apart, they should know that the place to go is the local church. This does not imply that the church will condone the behavior of the broken any more than Jesus approved of the woman's adultery or Zacchaeus's cheating the taxpayers, but it does mean that we will love and sustain the broken in Jesus' name.

It was late in the evening while I was sitting in a hospital waiting room. My father had undergone surgery earlier in the day, and I was staying the night with him. I had walked down the hall to the lobby and found a comfortable chair in the corner. The nurses were attending to Dad while I took a short break. While I was sitting there, someone came into the darkened lobby and took a seat. A little later the man said, "Aren't you Bob Morgan?" We struck up a conversation, and I discovered this was an outstanding Christian layman whom I had known when I was a teenager.

The conversation got around to each of us explaining why we were in the hospital. He said that he was sitting with a long-standing friend who was dying of cancer. He went on to say that the man had been in a terminal condition and at death's door for nearly six weeks. He also added that he had sat with him each evening during that period of time.

He said the man was not a Christian, but one of his close friends. He said that the man was his fishing buddy. In the darkness of that hospital lobby, he shared an experience that he had with his friend while they were fishing. The layman asked him why he had never joined the church. He said the man was a decent fellow, a good friend, and community leader, but never had anything to do with the church. He said he ventured on to ask him to give his life to Christ.

When he did this the friend retorted, "Don't ever say that to me again. . . . If I ever want to talk about giving my life to Christ, . . . I'll bring up the subject."

Tears welled up in the eyes of my old friend. He said, "That incident was several years ago. I have never brought the subject up since that time." He continued, "Now my friend has been in that hospital bed for six weeks, dying. Each day I go to my real estate office. In the evening I come out here and sit with him. In the mornings I go home and shower. I have breakfast with my wife and go to work and return to the hospital. I have been doing this for six weeks," he concluded, "hoping and praying that he will 'bring up the subject.' "

There are two attitudes that the church can take when confronted with the needs of the broken world. One attitude is *escape* and the other is *engage*.

We can choose to *escape,* turn away from cries—sometimes silent cries—of the broken and wash our hands of the matter much like Pontius Pilate. If this is our choice, we will discover that we cannot wash them clean.

Answering the call to follow Christ means to *engage* the world. To discover the needs of people and meet them. To find the hurts of the world and heal them. As the Father sent Jesus to witness to a broken world, he sends you and me.

As the Father sent Jesus to witness to a world in need, so he sends us. We are sent to serve a needy world, for the sake of others and for our own sake.

Jesus attempted time and time again to communicate his expectation that his followers be servants of the world. He made this known by what he said and did.

When the disciples were in an argument about greatness one day, Jesus said, "Whoever would be great among you must be a servant." He climaxed this by saying, "The son of man came not to be served but to serve, and to give his life." In other words, Jesus was saying there is no greater calling in the world than that of serving others.

Two of Jesus' choicest stories were on this theme. The first of these features a Samaritan and a man who was attacked by robbers. The victim was left dying beside the road. Two churchmen came by, but neither of them stopped to assist the wounded man. However, a Samaritan, detested by the Jews, was moved by the stranger's plight and stopped to help him. He administered first aid, converted his donkey into an ambulance, and took the victim to the nearest hostel where he arranged for his care.

The point of the story was plain: Jesus was illustrating the way of love. He was saying that high office in the church and correct belief about religion is not enough. Even the lawyer who stood there with a cocked ear could see that the only thing that really matters is a spirit of loving helpfulness.

In a day when so many people seem to feel that they are to be served and the world owes them a living, it is refreshing to recall this story about a man who served others because he felt he owed the world love.

The second story Jesus told makes the same point in an even more dramatic way. It is the parable of the Last Judgment. This parable is the subject of one of Michelangelo's great frescoes in the Sistine Chapel in Rome. A visitor to the Vatican will never forget Michelangelo's magnificent scene. The people are being separated by a righteous judge. Some go to the right, and some to the left. The serene expressions on some of the faces painted by the great artist and the violent gestures of others are dramatic evidence of the finality of the divine decision. And yet the decision is not based on the vindictive wrath of the judge. People's actions or inactions in their lives determined their fate. What was the principle of the separation? It was one question only. Did you help others in need? That's all there was to it. Someone was hungry. Did you feed them? Someone was thirsty. Did you give them something to drink? Someone was a stranger. Did you extend hospitality to them? Someone was dying. Did you comfort them? Someone was in prison. Did you visit them?

There is nothing in the story about whether a person subscribed to a certain creed or belonged to a certain church. There was nothing that said whether the person was of a certain race or nationality. The point of the story is painfully blunt. Did you serve the hungry, the thirsty, the lonely, the naked, the sick, the imprisoned? If so, come and stand with the righteous!

During the sixties, I was pastor of Forest Lake United Methodist Church in Tuscaloosa, Alabama. A number of historic events related to the civil rights movement took place during my days in Tuscaloosa. George Wallace made his infamous three-minute stand in the door denying a black student's enrollment in the University of Alabama. The school was integrated, and today, many people of Tuscaloosa wonder what all the uproar was about.

Many people contributed to the problems caused by racism by stubbornly holding on to the past. Others committed themselves to being advocates of justice in the community. The congregation at Forest Lake made a powerful witness for justice.

They did more than simply enter the debate. They discovered that there was a neighborhood of sixty houses occupied by black families that were denied basic services provided for other city dwellers. We discovered that there was one water faucet for the entire community. No indoor plumbing in any of the dwellings. Raw sewage ran unrestrained in the street. Interestingly, the street was named Grace Street.

The members of Forest Lake entered into a solidarity relationship with the people of Grace Street. They appealed the conditions to the insensitive landlord, as well as City Hall. We rented a couple of the houses and opened up a community center. Plumbing along with washers and dryers were installed for the convenience of the community. Recreation, child care, and tutoring services were established. Hundreds of members from the church participated in working with the residents to fix up and clean up the community.

Many from the Grace Street community began to attend church. They joined us for worship and community suppers and other occasions, and we attended their community and church functions to demonstrate our solidarity.

This reconciling ministry was going on during some of the most bleak times in the state's history. It did not go unnoticed by those who labeled our activity as unAmerican, unpatriotic, and treacherous. Not one time did anyone say that what we did was unlike Christ. After all, that is really all that counts.

One can never forget that disclosive scene in the Gospel according to John. It is the time of the Last Supper. The moments are pregnant with solemnity. As the disciples talk in muted tones, the Master rises from the table, secures a basin of water and a towel, and stoops to wash the feet of his followers. It is an act of lowly service. When he has finished, he says, "I have given you an example" (John 13:15).

Who can erase that picture from his or her mind? Here is the Lord of Life himself bending low and performing an act of menial service for the disciples who would, with one exception, forsake him in a few hours. By this example Jesus had toppled all our images of greatness. By this example he has declared that the greatest thing in the world is to serve others.

In the year A.D. 109, an aqueduct was built by the Roman legions in the city of Segovia, Spain. It was a magnificent piece of engineering. It continued in use for eighteen hundred years, serving the people of that city. Some years ago, however, the Spaniards decided that this ancient structure should be preserved for posterity and relieved of its centuries-old labor. So they laid modern pipelines, and the water ceased to gush through the old aqueduct. Soon it began to fall apart. The hot sun dried the mortar. The aqueduct crumbled and lay in ruins. As long as it served mankind, it was preserved, but when it ceased to be useful, it crumbled.

I have seen this happen to people. There are persons who start out with fine service motivation for their lives. But something happens. They begin to get greedy and self-concerned. Finally, they resent doing anything for other people if they do not receive a "return" for their investment. Whether they know it or not, their lives are lying in ruins, just as the Spanish aqueduct did when it no longer served human need.

Jesus knew that a person who lives only for themselves never lives, and a person who lives for others finds true fulfillment in life.

Finally, *as the Father sent Jesus to witness to a lost world, so he sends us.* We are sent to save a lost world.

Sometimes Christians have been careless in their use of the word *lost*. William Barkley reminded us that in the eyes of Jesus, to be lost meant simply to be in the wrong place. When we get lost in life, we merely get out of our own place and slip into the wrong place. In order to be found, we have to return to the place where we ought to be. In Christian terms, we get lost when we lose sight of what it means to be children of the Living God and wander away from him. Remember the great fifteenth chapter of the gospel according to Luke: it is all about the "lost" . . . a lost coin, a lost sheep, and two lost sons. To save is to find, to restore, to bring back to its rightful place what is lost.

Jesus made known in the story of Zacchaeus that he came "to seek and save what was lost." He certainly means lost souls, as in the case of Zacchaeus and the host of others he saved, but he also means structures and systems of a society that make life difficult for all of God's children.

Clement of Alexandria, one of the early Christian fathers, said this of Jesus, "He turns our sunsets into sunrises." Jesus was able to do that because he saw persons not in terms of the past failures and sins, but in terms of their future possibilities.

There are those who observe the way Jesus related to sinners and quickly conclude that it was not and is not a very sensible approach. There is an element of sheer foolhardiness in it. It is a rather risky way of dealing with people. But that is the way that Jesus related to people. By our standards, he took some silly risks and gambled on some unpromising people. Jesus related to all persons as children of God—persons of worth who were capable of responding to God's forgiveness and love, and therefore, salvation.

Look at Zacchaeus. If Jesus had displayed the kind of moral sensitivity we often display when we deal with the Zacchaeuses of our society, Zacchaeus would still be up in that tree. How willing are we to take risks for the outcasts of our society? How willing are we to risk our precious ingrown respectability in the cause of compassion and redemption?

Recently I preached on our need to take risks when it comes to the Zacchaeuses of our community. Following the service, a middle-aged man waited around until most of the congregation had gone. He walked up to me and said, "I am the one you were talking about in your sermon. This congregation rescued me when I was dying." He then went on to explain that he had been a successful professional and had allowed alcohol to ruin his life. He lost his job, marriage, family, and self-respect. He went on to say, "I am here today because those people took a chance on me when no one cared. They stood by me and have walked with me through my recovery. I am more alive today than I have been in my forty-six years." I have never been more proud of any congregation.

Can it be said of us that we in the church have become so institutionalized and culturalized that we have lost our compassion for what is lost? Jesus has sent us out to be witnesses of his saving love. We are to be concerned for the lost ones and, in the spirit of Jesus, help bring them home again where they belong.

I remember reading about a New York City giftshop. A sign in the window read, "Huge Jigsaw Puzzle Bargain . . . Original Price $39.95 . . . Now only $2.95." Then in fine print was the explanation for this fantastic bargain, "Three pieces missing."

At a 93 percent discount, the bargain can't be matched in any store. Yet, there were three irreplaceable pieces missing. Not one of the other 4,997 remaining pieces could ever fill the places of those missing pieces or complete the magnificent painting the puzzle was to portray. Three missing pieces! Only three! Yet these gaps reduced the value of the puzzle and rendered it incomplete.

Jesus sends us to witness to the lost ones of life who have wandered off from God and are in the wrong places. Until the lost come home the picture is incomplete. Not until they are found will God's picture become whole. Seems like Jesus said something about a hundred sheep and one was lost . . . Jesus has made it known that we are to witness to a lost world by issuing an invitation on his behalf. Jesus said, "You will be my witnesses to the very ends of the earth. As the Father sent me, so I send you."